AS FOR ME AND MY BODY
A Memoir of Sinclair Ross

AS FOR ME AND MY BODY

A Memoir of Sinclair Ross

KEATH FRASER

ECW PRESS

CANADIAN CATALOGUING IN PUBLICATION DATA

Fraser, Keath

As for me and my body : a memoir of Sinclair Ross

ISBN 1-55022-310-0

1. Ross, Sinclair, 1908– . – Last years.
2. Authors, Canadian (English) – 20th century –
Biography.*   I. Title.

PS8535.079Z63 1997   C813´54   C96-932459-6
PR9199.3.R599Z63 1997

Imaging by ECW Type & Art, Oakville, Ontario.
Printed by Printcrafters Inc., Winnipeg, Manitoba.

Distributed in Canada by General Distribution Services,
30 Lesmill Road, Don Mills, Ontario M3B 2T6.

Published by ECW PRESS,
2120 Queen Street East, Suite 200,
Toronto, Ontario M4E 1E2.

http://www.ecw.ca/press

for

Rod McGillis

Actually the creative experience lies so unbelievably close to the sexual, close to its pain and its pleasure, that both phenomena are only different forms of the same longing and bliss.

— Rainer Maria Rilke

I

When Jim Ross came to live in Vancouver in March 1982, he was worried about two things: losing his independence and losing his mind. For the next three years and four months he clung precariously to his independence, then fell and broke his hip, after which he never lived on his own again. He had fallen once before, not many weeks after his arrival, when a vicious little war of attrition going on in his brain had blackened his will to live. I happened to observe this war close by, and on that earlier occasion wiped up the blood. But it was another eight years until he confided to me what really happened the day I found him wandering in his bedroom slippers, bruised and battered, in a sandwich shop on Denman Street.

We'd discussed suicide more than once that spring, when the Sinemet he was taking to control his tremors was releasing too much dopamine into the brain, developing in him periodic hallucinations and delusions typical of schizophrenic behaviour. He never talked in this doctorly way, but instead he spoke of how the dopamine he lacked naturally often made him feel "grim" and "suicidal." He would mention the "noises" he was hearing. Or rather, to be more accurate about these sounds, how many of his own noises the woman in the apartment above his would allow him before she started "knocking" on his ceiling in reprimand; before she began "mimicking" some sound of his she couldn't possibly have heard in order, he believed, to mock him.

The war advanced. "She" became his obsession, though in some ways this pronoun had been with my friend all his life, in the slightly dismissive, perhaps misogynist way of someone once forced to live with a domineering woman and to support her for far longer than was healthy. "After living with Mother for most of my life, I couldn't face living with anybody again," he told me years later, about someone who once offered to live with him in Athens. A few months before his death he was to confess his mother had made him a snob. Now he was reluctant to type, play his records, drop a pencil on the floor. He kept his curtains closed and the blossoms out. "I'd just like to slip away." Fearful and depressed, intermittently confused, he experienced nightmares and trouble sleeping. He heard voices. And he began to answer these voices when things got blackest. He was holding on, persistent in his independence, a guerrilla fighter in his own mind since childhood.

I could recall an earlier letter from Montreal, before he left there to come west, in which he complained that he was "having apartment trouble . . . noise and more noise. The neighbours object to *my* noise, the electric typewriter, so I have to keep it to a minimum." In Vancouver he began to harbour the legitimate worry that his problem might go deeper than a change of cities could cure. Having contracted Parkinson's disease in the late 1970s, while living in Spain, he'd returned to Montreal for better treatment in his declining years. He was still hoping for a better life when he arrived in Vancouver and tried settling into a pleasant apartment up against the rhododendrons of Stanley Park. He was seventy-four that year. When he died on leap year day, 1996, of pneumonia at age eighty-eight, he had been suffering from Parkinson's for almost twenty years.

It wasn't that his mental state prevented him from being lucid and congenial. Our conversations ranged widely, over books we were reading, magazines shared, and especially over his past and present life. He might talk at length about an old friend like Forbes Murray, a shallow but charming preacher, for whom he'd played the organ in small towns around Arcola, Saskatchewan, and who went on to become a Mountie in the musical ride. "Mother thought the world of Forbes!" So did the girls, said Jim. Years later he'd heard that Forbes, too, had contracted Parkinson's.

My friend could be good company and on occasion even enjoy meeting other people in spite of understandable misgivings about his disability, his reluctance to be seen shaking, or cutting his meat. "A kind of inverted vanity I guess." He could sometimes tell a joke in company, and then his whole face slowly lost its Parkinsonian "mask," the lines at his eyes began to crinkle, cheeks pumped mirthfully, and mouth fell open so his long upper lip lost its customary stiffness to allow his eye teeth to peek through a loose, goofy smile. A small whinny of laughter might even, at the punch line, escape him. For a while he could forget the bleakness inside, bleakness bred in the child.

Then he would remember this child, a kind of orphan that ran through much of his fiction and in fact through himself. Large ears and a small stature had limited his self-esteem so far back it seemed he was born to an inverted self-deprecation. It was useful for him to carry on compromising with this abiding insecurity by seldom overvaluing himself, at least not in public. Most who met him remarked on his characteristic "modesty." Indeed, he'd perfected a manner of flushing out the prairie "hick" by playfully acknowledging that fellow, although this didn't entirely disguise an underlying vanity or wilfulness. While cultivating sympathy for the once lonely child — to whose humiliating predicament he'd never quite reconciled himself — he exacted at the same time admiration for the precocious child he'd been. Thus while admitting to gullibility, he also prided himself on being "sharp" enough to "spot" anyone who might try to "get around" him. "I'm a credulous person by nature," he'd confessed years before in Athens. That was in 1970. "But when you get old, you know, you get a little cautious. I don't like to stick my neck out. I've had it chopped too many times."

In his early sixties then, he seemed a curious mixture of candour and caution, faintly comical to a pair of admiring travellers in their twenties. Nothing cavalier or outspoken threatened to betray this most non-authorly of writers. His relief at our youth appeared palpable and revealing. As did a slight sense of shame and regret for having pushed, perhaps too hard, for a contract he now felt free to celebrate with us in a fancy pastry shop — for a film option he'd received that day for his first novel, thirty years after publication. He was wondering if its absence of a covering letter reflected unflatteringly on his having quibbled too much over terms. "But you can't be too careful you know." His caution in general seemed to blind him to how much of himself he'd once revealed in his fiction. About the relationship of his parents, for instance, he seemed unaccountably sensitive. "It doesn't come out in the stories does it?" A quarter century ago it was like talking to a man freshly acquainted with Freud and the nature of family imprinting. He seemed unable to understand the world except in personal terms, which he preferred at the same time to disavow.

Never entirely trustful of those even closest to him, he was a lifelong pessimist shaped by circumstance and an inherited Presbyterian-Unitarianism on his mother's side, bred in the pulpits of Scotland, where at age twenty-eight his grandfather (Fraser by name) had collapsed and died preaching, he told me in Spain. Sometimes in later years it was difficult to tell just how much to attribute his bedevilled view of himself in the world to the strong pills he was taking, and how much to his obliquely complex nature which seldom forgot a slight or permitted him much elation. When he put on his thick glasses to read a menu, with his poker face cultivated years before, he could look as severe as a judge with piles.

At any rate, you listened that spring when "she" or somebody else he believed to be persecuting him entered the conversation, causing him to wonder whether or not he was wanted in his own building after all. He did not think he would last long living by himself, unsettled as things were. "I'm worried that I can't cope." His tendency to panic was what worried him. Even within a week or two of his arrival on the West Coast we were discussing nursing homes, Long Term Care, homemakers. By the end of May he was still disconcertingly rational about the irrational. He had decided to see a psychiatrist. Down on himself and brooding dangerously, he worried he was paranoid. If anything happened to him, he went on, I was to remember to do this and that. And he thanked me for being a good friend. This was the last time I saw him until after his fall two or three days later.

When I found him staggering that June afternoon in the sandwich shop, I thought of a failed attempt on his own life. He was ashen. We were alone. The huge bruise above his eye attested to the fall he said he'd suffered. Mumbling, he mentioned that his psychiatrist had rescheduled an appointment he should have had yesterday, his first. In its place the nurse had asked him to take notes about the knocking business, in order to have a better idea of whether he really was hearing the noises he claimed were bothering him. He was feeling beset, helpless.

Only after returning with him by taxi from St. Paul's Emergency — and then cleaning up the blood on the parquet floor of his apartment, sorting through splattered clothes in the bathroom, stripping his pillowcase, and listening to the explanation of his slipping in the bath and then crawling for his phone, before blacking out at about two a.m. —

did I think a "fall" made more sense than a failed attempt at suicide. His wounds attested to a fall. You didn't commit suicide by throwing yourself on the floor. Did you? I thought afterwards I should have paid more attention to a note I recalled noticing inside the plastic lid of his record player.

But I was listening to him reminiscing on the couch about how Dutch Cleanser was one of his earliest memories. The hospital experience had perked him up. The X-rays had revealed no broken bones and he wasn't concussed. He recalled the ring of blue-bonneted ladies chasing dirt with sticks around old Dutch Cleanser cans. The next day I brought him over a rubber mat for his tub. And in the following weeks and months we went on meeting as before, having lunches and long talks, going to films and an occasional concert at the Orpheum, picnicking that summer and the next at Locarno Beach, enjoying dinners at our apartment or at restaurants he'd found on his own.

His mental state improved somewhat, although occasionally he might lose his temper and curse his failed life as a writer. And he still heard voices. One voice in his dreams kept accusing him of spying for Moscow. It actually forced him to get up one morning and take out his passport to prove he'd never been to Moscow. He told me about this recurrent nightmare two days after Anthony Blunt died. Donald Maclean, incidentally, had died in Moscow the week before. He bought himself a new lamp, considered getting a TV if he could listen through an earphone, and decided he sometimes liked his curtains open.

For a time he started going to a Parkinson's support group, mingling a bit with others similarly afflicted, and he could be darkly wry about his predicament. I remember sitting with him over coffee in a now (mercifully) defunct café called Funky's, when he said he'd heard somewhere that filling your mouth with water, before blowing out your brains, made your head explode like a balloon. But he had no gun. In truth he was a tidy, meticulous man who hated mess instinctively. He had now begun to see his psychiatrist.

It was to be a bad year for men who lived alone and never married, having stayed close to their mothers. In November the great Canadian sprinter Percy Williams, hero of the 1928 Olympic games in Amsterdam, shot himself through the head in a bathtub just up the street. If Ross and I talked at all about this suicide we didn't linger over symptoms. "You feel like dirty water," he'd said the month before of his own disease. "Your *skin* feels like dirty water, hanging on you." By November he was still feeling "rocky."

A year and a half after his first fall, things remained intermittently threatening for him. "I feel like the Sword of Damocles is over my head." A year and a half after that, another fall, in July 1985, broke his hip and finally cost him his independence. A sadly ironical fate, because lying on the floor of his fifth-floor apartment for twenty-four hours, tapping as loudly as he could on the wall with a stick, no one in the building including "her" heard his noise. Once hospitalized he never returned to his apartment and spent his remaining eleven years in extended care.

It was typical of Ross to take the long view of friendship. "I never told you this before," he confided in 1990, eight years after falling the first time, when this fall came up in conversation: "I tried to kill myself." He was belted into a wheelchair now, like the other patients in rooms around us. "A bottle of gin and aspirin." Pause. "I was in bad shape, because of the new dosage of medicine my doctor in Montreal put me on." Pause. "I even tried to buy a gun. I went out looking for one."

By then he was past his suicidal stage, and enjoying life a little more than he would admit, in a nursing home for overseas vets where he was well taken care of and where he'd begun to write again. His dosage of medicine slowly reached a more balanced state, although in these later years he was never entirely free of turmoil and nightmares, or of an occasional sense of persecution. It went without saying that he felt neglected and overlooked, in spite of increasing attention to his work and a growing circle of friends and admirers. Enthusiasm, of course, he kept firmly in its place. "I'm the most pessimistic person alive." His audience had come too late to make any difference, he felt, which perhaps accounted for an increasing addiction to praise. He felt perceptibly diminished when he was not the centre of attention. "I'm susceptible to praise," he once admitted. He wasn't the simple man he liked to let on. Except for brief periods of genuine tranquillity, he never overcame an innate sense of failure. Nor, in truth, of hope. "I haven't made up my mind about it yet," he confided that same year, talking about the after-life. "One thing I'm sure of, I won't be punished. Nothing we might have done is worth being punished for."

What I want to highlight is how his first fall had signalled a shift in our friendship. If he was reluctant earlier on to divulge the truth about the cause of it, he did finally begin to talk to me of other things.

★ ★ ★

Homosexuality in literature and life was a natural topic of conversation for two writers, one of them gay, one of them (me) curious about why the other should remain circumspect about being gay, when conceal-ment seemed more richly left to the metaphors of fiction. In the spring of 1982 I had mentioned to him *The Great Gatsby*, a novel I'd written about in another career in order to demonstrate how neatly Fitzgerald had kept sixty years of readers in the dark over his narrator's true sexuality. Such secrecy seemed to me a wonderful metaphor for fiction itself. At the time, all Jim would say was, "I suppose a man would write that way whether he knew he was one or not." A homosexual, he meant.

We'd been chewing over the "intentional fallacy" at lunch, and he conceded that sometimes one of the numerous critics of his work could point out some-thing he hadn't recognized himself. Still, he claimed, an essay on the Bible and his first novel had gone too far; despite what people thought, he really didn't know the Bible well at all, so what was the use of pretending he did. On this occasion he preferred to talk (a little shyly) about oral sex. I think he was skeptical of V.S. Naipaul's denigration of macho men in Argentina, the subject of a recent essay by Naipaul. Jim had a soft spot for macho men.

He could be very frank in his talk about sex, almost daring himself to see how far he might go. But it usually stopped short of personal revelations. He might remember how the daughter of a fellow banker had once asked her father if he (the father) was gay. I would then ask if he recalled Susan Cheever's asking her father the same question in a *Newsweek* interview after the novel *Falconer* appeared. On another occasion he might urge me to read the recent David Leavitt story in *The New Yorker*, a beautiful story he thought, and go on to say how he once thought of writing a similar story from the father's point of view, about the "shame and guilt" this father felt for producing a homosexual son. No, it wasn't that he didn't talk frankly about homosexuals and indirectly about himself. But he was careful.

"Everybody's homosexual these days," he said one day, acknowledging a novel on my coffee table. "Everybody's coming out of the closet." He then mentioned a coffee shop on Davie where he'd been sitting at the counter. "There were a couple of boys sitting across the way. I was pretty sure they were [*sic*]. Then all of a sudden one boy wet his finger like this and leant over towards the other boy and wiped something off his lips." He mimed for me the licking, leaning, wiping. Later he returned to what he called the "homoerotic" in Fitzgerald's work. He was clearly thinking about our earlier discussion: about, I suspected, himself. But clouded with other concerns he was in no rush to compound these with the anxiety any intimate revelation might involve. At the same time I think he hoped to discover I was gay, before committing himself to some fuller disclosure about himself. (He never quite came to believe that I, and any other male in whom he might be physically interested, were quite so straight we couldn't be tempted by the pleasures available in a male body, or that such a body wasn't part of every man's fantasies. He was pretty sure it was. This might even explain his supposition that a man might "write that way whether he knew he was one or not.")

It was understandable for a man of his generation and background to take some time to emerge from the self-protective habit of a lifetime. He was not an aggressively secretive man, just cautious and mildly deceptive in the manner of the banker he'd been for nearly fifty years. I could recall his telling my wife and me in Athens, where we met him after his retirement from the Royal Bank, how he sometimes longed for a little female company and how the Greek social system forbade him this as a confirmed bachelor. I recall him saying the character of Paul Kirby in his first novel was based on a girl he knew. (It was, of course, a kind of self-portrait that he would readily admit to in later years.) And he went on a little boyishly about the girls in Piraeus, where a happy group of whores had propositioned him, amusing both themselves and him when he promised to come back the next day.

He came to prefer Spain to Greece, Lorca to Cavafy I suppose, and moved to Barcelona not long after he published his third novel later that same year. *Whir of Gold*, set in Montreal, was forced and unsuccessful, though he clung to the belief that it wasn't a bad book given its limited range. This limited range happened to include the heterosexual relationship of two young people like ourselves, aliens really, eating dolmathes with him. He tended to take on the colours of his surroundings, and not be fully aware of the extent to which these might not be his colours.

Perhaps this is why I thought he might find Vancouver's West End a good place to live, with its interesting cross-section of people, including a sizeable gay population. I was wrong. He confessed he felt like he was living in a picture postcard, unable as a son of the bald prairie to appreciate the rich contending colours of this new landscape. (He once tried a walk around the lagoon in Stanley Park but lost his balance, banged his head, and never went back.) He was curious about the indigenous gay population, although any acknowledgement of his own colours in conversation seemed a slow if not unflirtatious dance. It would still be another half-dozen years — after opening the closet on himself with me in the sandwich shop that smashed-up afternoon — before he eventually got rid of the closet door. That was when things got more intimate, but also more undignified. It was as though Philip in his first novel, the constant shutter of that most famous door in our literature, had suddenly got loose with a crowbar.

It was an odd conversation in the Denman Street sandwich shop, mugged as he had just been by the excessive dopamine in his brain. I see now how this recent trauma, along with the sense of a botched conclusion to his life, could have finally overcome his characteristic reticence about certain personal matters and prompted him to tidy up unfinished business — now that he'd been given a second, if unwelcome, chance.

★ ★ ★

When I returned to our table from phoning for a cab, he began to pour out in a small, self-pitying voice things that had nothing apparently to do with his present crisis. "You know. I used to be excessively attracted to good-looking young men, when I was young. No more. They mean nothing now . . . Too old." He indicated a young man who had come in moments earlier and ordered a sandwich. "Sometimes you couldn't control the feeling."

His mumbling ran on like an elegy. "There was a case of an important politician in Spain," he said weakly, "who was attracted to a young boy. He knew what the consequences of his actions would be. He went ahead, anyway. Ruined his career. It's a feeling you can't control . . ." Like a fall, I supposed later, sex and violence seeming linked in his mind as they often had been in his fiction.

At the hospital a little later, just before he was led away for X-rays, he continued: "This morning I thought of 'The Flowers That Killed Him.' You know. Falling forwards, the legs out from under him . . ." He was alluding to a short story he had published a decade earlier, in which a sex murderer who preys on adolescent boys tumbles to his death from a fifth-floor balcony. (It never occurred to me at the time of choosing it for him that his own apartment on Comox, with the balcony he refused to use, was also on the fifth floor.) He was now sitting in a green hospital gown with dignity and quietude. Surprising to us both were his tremors: they'd stopped. Beaten up and badly bruised he suddenly looked cured. A catharsis? Or resignation to things now out of his control and beyond him? In the taxi to the hospital he'd confided: "Hospitals terrify me. Until I'm inside. Then I feel safe. I feel taken care of. They're like a train."

But he was also speaking of euthanasia. "When you don't have anyone anymore what's the point? You're young," he said. "You have friends. I don't have anybody." Waiting there, we overheard a young male doctor in the cubicle alongside ours administering to a loud alcoholic mother, his odd but speedy psychiatric counselling for depression: *"What single, overwhelming thing matters to you at this point in time?"* He was berating her, intentionally impatient, trying to jolt her with an electric verbal shock, before softening the wattage in his voice: "What do you look forward to?" Jim's immediate response, mocking himself a little, *"The New Yorker."*

I left him alone to eavesdrop. It might help to hear he wasn't by any means alone in misery. Later, in our taxi going home, he said nothing of the woman in crisis. Instead: "That doctor must have been an awfully intelligent young man." Doctors fascinated him (he'd created two of them in novels) and so did bodies: how they worked, who took care of them, and in particular what had happened to his own. I can remember his deep interest that spring in whether or not his having had Spanish Flu in childhood could possibly have contributed to his present disease in old age. And I'd sometimes wondered if the odd gait or sidle I first noticed when he was hailing a Greek taxi in Omonia Square could have been some foreshadowing of his Parkinson's. It was ignorant speculation on my part, valueless, except for how he responded.

He was silent, apparently fascinated. This was years after our ride home that day from hospital. He seemed more taken by my observation of his body than by any linkage of limp to disease. (Almost as if no one had ever noticed his gait before — rather unlikely — like not noticing his gayness when he spoke about or looked at waiters.) He then said he was going to tell me something he'd never told anyone else. But not about his present disease. From his wheelchair he confided that he'd walked in an odd manner since childhood, and that in the army his drill sergeant, "the bastard, made my life hell." Later on, rereading his story "Jug and Bottle," I saw where Jim had given his suicide, Coulter, precisely this ungainly walk on the parade ground where the

NCOs yell and make fun of him: "His neck was long, his nose a beak, his shoulders weak and drooping. His self-consciousness inclined him to hurry, like a nervous horse; then, to keep in step with the rest of the men, he had to hold back a little, so that he seemed to hesitate slightly every time he brought his foot down."

His body, yes. A body that even before Parkinson's started shaking it — *in*side as well as out, imprisoning him so the whole structure made you want to die, according to another notable victim, Bill Reid — his body had been an intermittent source of shame and torment since childhood. This, though, hadn't stopped him from being understandably vain about parts of it: for example, his long slim hands and how he used them to gesture or to move gracefully over piano keys. (And he was downright narcissistic about another part of his anatomy, which not to notice presently would be to ignore his body entirely.) In later years he even started experimenting with alternative therapy to improve his visage, by staring into the mirror in order to *think* his looks better than they appeared. And before he entered hospital he'd always dressed his body well, in good suits and fine shoes and button-down collars. An underweight body in banker's clothing. The spring he came to Vancouver he weighed 102 pounds and hated to wear a short-sleeved shirt because he thought his arms looked like "spindles." Appearances mattered and they continued to interest him. False fronts fascinated him. He could relax behind these, which he never could behind his Parkinson's.

"Telling lies is as natural as camouflage," he said. "White lies. To protect yourself."[*]

Indeed, he was first attracted to writing fiction in the series of false-fronted towns he began to live in with his mother when she retired from housekeeping on farms. She never did believe in his fiction. And the son — after she'd decided he was to be a respectable young bank clerk following his grade eleven education — never believed in hers. Her respectable hypocrisy was correct but it wasn't necessarily right for a budding artist. A career in banking had nothing to do with the imagination he'd been cultivating with books and her connivance since childhood.

I sometimes think his first and most important novel, *As for Me and My House* (1941), might be called *As for Me and My Body*, because this is what I believe it really concerns — at an obsessive, unadmitted level — a revelation of its author's deepest desires and fears, and is partly what prompts my selective memoir, the false front of this novel and his other fiction about which much literary criticism has ignored the body in question.

No broken bones, no concussion . . . but I mentioned that. The day following our hospital visit in 1982 he was already entertaining a suggestion that

---

[*]   Among these white lies or false fronts, I suppose, could be counted the facelift he'd had in Spain. Since finishing my memoir I've heard from David Stouck that Jim had once revealed this bit of cosmetic surgery to John O'Connor. I am struck by just how far the interest in his own body had come over the years.

he try taping his memoirs. I thought it might settle his mind a little by focusing on what interested him increasingly, the past. Having opened up yesterday about his physical lusts, he now seemed in a memoir-ish mood, even a good mood. He said he'd have to be very honest about himself, tell a lot about himself. He was speaking to me now in confidence.

It sounded like a test run, minus his typewriter, which he was reluctant to use for fear of making noise. He spoke of his childhood — how he'd made a conscious decision to retreat from the "ugliness" of life at the age of nine or ten, into a "fantasy world." He'd built "a shell around himself." He talked about what it had been like to "be baited" by other boys — not least because of the way his mother dressed him in shorts and frilly shirts to show other mothers she was better than them. He was clearly unhappy remembering his mother yet resigned to her superior ways. She had scarred him by her dominance. She had betrayed him at least once by telling him to lie about his absent father being dead, which he did, before schoolmates found out the truth through what Mrs. Ross had told their mothers.

He recalled attending a picnic once, standing all day beside a tree, not taking part in games because the boys in dungarees would have laughed at him. He remembered the awful rage he felt toward boys who baited him. Did he have a bad temper? "Oh yes." The past now seemed more present than the present. He'd read voraciously from a young age. "Books were all I had." Enlarging on much of what I'd already heard in cafés and living rooms with him, my friend was trying out his memory in a more formal, therapeutic way than was usual when the dialogue went back and forth.

I could remember him pulling down a biography of Lorca from his bookcase, a month earlier, and his identifying with Lorca whom he adored as a writer and man, but to whom recognition had come easily in a way it hadn't come to Sinclair Ross. It was now June. Later that month John Cheever would die, a *New Yorker* writer Jim had been reading for as long as Cheever had been publishing stories in that magazine. Not only was everybody coming out of the closet, as he'd observed, they were also dying off. So he was in good company if he should ever decide to go public before his own demise.

But it was not himself he was to make public — but "Mother." The only memoir he would publish was a brief one several years later, at an invitation to contribute to the first *Macmillan Anthology* my friends John Metcalf and Leon Rooke were then editing. Jim seized the opportunity to contribute to it in a characteristically cautious and circuitous way. Not consenting right away, he nevertheless began writing the piece in his head and in shorthand, trying it out, before pecking a bit on a small typewriter I brought him one day, and then, when the keys got too stiff for him to press, dictating to me from memory the second paragraph of his story with its punctuation included.

The subject was one he knew intimately. Over the next few months he worked and reworked thirty typewritten pages with his amanuensis, Irene

Harvalias. It was written with enough dialogue, rhythm, and imagery to be a piece of fiction. Indeed, it was a piece of fiction: a lively, nuanced evocation of his mother's world as he recalled it, which narrated only a little of the resentment he felt toward a woman he regarded as jealous, self-centred, cruel, and once (still) an impediment to his freedom. His working title had been "The Unreliable Narrator," a reference to the fashionable view of the narrator of his first novel. But who was the narrator here? (Who was it there?) He thought better of this, since deep down he never believed Mrs. Bentley was "unreliable" or "manipulative" in the way she'd been portrayed by critics, and he wasn't sure the allusion would be picked up or was worth picking up. He readily accepted one of his editor's suggestions to call his story what — as he'd revealed in it — his mother had thought of his fiction: "Just Wind and Horses."

In this memoir he was quietly interested in redressing the balance of a radio documentary his friend Ken Mitchell had made about his life in which he felt the slant "was hard on Mother." It was mainly his mother's memory that concerned him — though I don't believe it was this documentary that motivated him so much as his own portrait of Benny Fox's monstrous mother and possible suicide in *Sawbones Memorial* (and even Philip's mother in his first novel: "Towards even her memory he remained implacable"). I suspect his own imbalance was the real balance he hoped to redress. Generally more correct than generous, he preferred, in the case of his family, to err on the side of generosity when he knew he was being false. He often told me he didn't care what people said about him after his own death, though he showed he did care by cooperating with his biographers, and by sometimes worrying over how long his widely studied novel would "be around." (He didn't mind fishing for what he expected to be compliments, even as senility advanced and pride in his appearance slowly deteriorated.)

During the writing of this memoir he worried whether he was being "fair" to his mother's memory. In truth, I think the memory he'd always wanted to be fair to was his father's, but because he barely knew his father before his mother took him away from the family as a young child, he spent the rest of his life making up idealized male protagonists with whom he identified more than with his female antagonists, who were sometimes better realized but more drab. It was his mother, for better or worse, who would be linked to him forever. It was *her* self-centred use and subtle resentment of him, he once confessed to me, that led to his abiding and emotional sense of illegitimacy.

That memoir was his only piece of published writing done in the years he lived in Vancouver, and it was, besides being an exceptional piece of work, therapeutic for him. It encouraged him to start another memoir, to contribute to an anthology on writers' worst journeys I was editing, though he later abandoned this project, after it had taken him much farther than the shorter piece on his mother had. His four-and-a-half-day voyage across the Atlantic in 1942 — hammocked like a sardine inside the library of the Queen Elizabeth, one of twenty-two thousand Canadian troops aboard this ocean liner — he decided was only stage one of an extended memoir he began to plan of their landing and deployment in the U.K. His ambition for it seemed to grow beyond his capacity to hold it all in mind. His short-hand-amended pages littered shelves and floor of his small room. He began to talk of it as a work of fiction. Perhaps he even hoped to redeem himself and the war novel he'd begun in London and later destroyed — a little precipitously he now thought — after a couple of hundred pages. (The bank he said had given him six months off to write it after the war, after he'd transferred from Winnipeg to Montreal, but he "couldn't do it." He wouldn't publish another novel until 1958.)

He was used to abandoning manuscripts. "It's all over anyway," he would say, by now nearing the end of his life. Like all real writers he needed to write as he needed to breathe, yet such passion wasn't something the part-time writer could admit to (and he didn't) for fear of hubris. Now he let his writing slip away; then gradually his reading; and finally his music, listening to it and playing it. His playing the communal hospital piano had stopped about the time his writing stopped. And his standard line became: "In many ways my life as a writer has been a failure, but it's been worth it."

It was the last false front he needed to keep up, if only for his biographers. David Stouck and John O'Connor helped him hold on for longer than he otherwise might have with their kind and professional interest in his life. And for the most part he looked forward to visits from people attracted to him and his work. Then when his voice grew weak and indistinct you often had to listen without understanding what he was telling you. "I'm beat," he whispered. "Used up." By then he was. Visitors fell off. So did his tremors, often in abeyance now. His deep brown eyes would sometimes take on their haunted, dilated death watch. No longer himself, he caused you to wonder at times who exactly he was when he had been himself. In these declining years you expected mood swings from visit to visit; and yet the man I visited in Spain, before his Parkinson's and the drugs began, wasn't the same man I remembered from Greece either. You came to feel that when his dignity faltered at times, even his reserve, he always managed to retain a sense of mystery, as though the condition of friendship couldn't survive without it. He knew this, and I admired him for it.

"This is a memoir about my mother," he had written, "a woman as difficult to describe as she was to live with. You never understood her; there were too many contradictions." Indeed, in spite of the hundreds of times I saw him over the years, the many confidences we shared, I think his words were also true of the son. He resisted summary. He took his own measure from a world often foreign to his, the straight world or else another country's culture, and seldom let on that a crisis of identity had been his abiding condition since childhood. "Old age, though — they at least give the impression of handling it better," he'd written to me from Barcelona in the early seventies. His observations of the Spaniard and the Greek were idealistic on the one hand, deflationary on the other: "And even before old age: a youth, then a young man, then a middle-aged one, then old — he always seems to know where he is — never a crisis of identity. . . . But of course, the moment you say something like that, you think of the exceptions — for instance the middle-aged Latin, and Greek, male — often inordinately vain — pulling in his paunch, slicking down what's left of his hair and strutting in front of the girls to let them see what they're passing up. . . ." The Mediterranean male had given him (as it had E.M. Forster) the model to cherish as well as avoid. Turning his picture upside down, as Philip Bentley suggests, knocked the sentiment out of "these little Main Streets" and let the artist really see them. Still, crisis of identity was the occupational hazard. Sinclair Ross *was* a difficult man to describe. He was more difficult to "read" than any other person I've known. And yet he often wondered, amid his own memories and associations, how others read his work.

2

One day ten years before his death, Ross asked me if I thought *As for Me and My House* was a homosexual novel. Before I could respond, a nurse, like some firm reminder sent by his mother, came into his room to suggest we all take a walk to exercise the patient.

Alone again later, I said yes, I had sometimes thought of his novel as homosexual — but only in terms of some hidden, maybe enriching metaphor as in *Gatsby*. I knew he would remember our conversations from four years earlier about Fitzgerald, even as I was forgetful of details in his own novel. Vague and cautious, hoping not to scare off any disclosure he wished to make about his work, I waited. He asked if I thought Paul was the father of Judith's child. No, I didn't see Paul as the father of Judith's child. He agreed. He also said he hadn't thought of his novel in homosexual terms. It was an odd, relaxed conversation. I think Philip, husband and adulterer in the novel, was on his mind.

For the first time since our sandwich-shop conversation in 1982, I then circled back to the fall he'd had and his revelation about lusting after young men. "When was that?" he asked, meaning when had he fallen. I thought perhaps he didn't want to talk about it and refrained from pressing him. After a while he said, "It's true. I did feel a sort of attraction to young men. Not that I was ever very active." Pause. "I was naïve. I never knew what a blowjob was till I was in my twenties."

Later that summer I took him James Baldwin's overtly homosexual novel *Giovanni's Room*. On a subsequent visit I discovered he was hiding it in a lower drawer. A lifetime of caution did not disappear overnight. He hadn't much liked the novel, he said, claiming it wasn't very well written. Evidently he'd only skimmed it (a little like another friend who only read *Playboy* for the articles). I should add that his not liking books recommended to him was more or less routine. It was as though he disagreed with Frye's stricture that you didn't raise your standards by limiting your taste — in Jim's case, taste for other people's preferences. He hadn't much cared for Frye either when they met in Toronto in 1941. Frye had taken him to a "gay" French restaurant where, according to Ross, the young academic made a presumptuous remark.

A year and a half later we were talking about Patrick White's autobiography. Under too much strain ever to write fiction again, Jim said he was again thinking of an autobiography. I knew that years ago he'd once tried writing his autobiography, piling up half an inch of manuscript before abandoning it, he said, finding the writing "too painful." The piece on his mother he didn't think he'd bother to include. He wanted to find a shape and perhaps begin *in medias res*. Would he tell any secrets? "There's always the presence of Mrs. Grundy," he pointed out. Then said he supposed everyone went through a compulsive masturbating stage. (He sometimes showed perceptible guilt about masturbation, hoping to hear once more from a friend or his doctor that masturbating was perfectly normal.) He alluded to White's account of his relationship with his male lover. And he related an intimate moment of White's in a taxi, when a woman sucked him off. He didn't like *Voss*, incidentally, for the same reason he didn't like *Under the Volcano*, say. He "didn't get it."

One book he did get and enjoy was a memoir by John Lehmann, published in 1971, on Christopher Isherwood. I knew he had met the homosexual Lehmann in a London pub during the war. (He'd also met Ezra Pound's son in the shower at the Y, where he often went, along with other "boys" of different nationalities. Pound's son was a rat-like man whose snobbishness he didn't care for, but agreed to meet him for "tea" several times. Jim long considered London during the war the great event of his life and never wanted it to end. He'd heard T.S. Eliot lecture and de Gaulle speak. He'd attended concerts, plays, the ballet. At the opera he had met a relative of Maynard Keynes's, and such people had sometimes extended him invitations to their homes. Best of all he'd escaped his mother, who was furious at him for enlisting.) The point was he loved Isherwood's writing. "When I read the Berlin stories I thought they were marvelous. Simple, clean. And he didn't apologize for his homosexuality."

Shortly after this, following on from a discussion about his mother, he casually asked me one day if anyone had thought of him as a homosexual writer. No one that I knew about, I answered. Did he wish they would? No, he was just as content to remain undisturbed now — "out of the limelight." But with Jim you knew how long he could ponder such a question before revealing "what was on his mind." At such times he didn't object to being prompted. I think I brought up Scott Fitzgerald again, as well as what he'd asked me a couple of years earlier about *As for Me and My House* being a homosexual novel. If I expected him to pick up on this I was mistaken.

Instead, to my surprise, he began to divulge a history of his sex life, in great detail, about particular "boys" he'd "had" in Montreal. And this he followed up with more general talk about all-male cinemas in Athens and Spain, where you could go for a hand- or blowjob. "I don't like fat," he allowed. And so it began. In a calm and confiding voice.

In the months and then years that followed, I was to hear about numerous other sexual encounters, often more than once. "Yes," he would tell me rather proudly, "I've seen a lot of low life." He'd become obsessed with sex, at least with talking about it, as if some powerful aphrodisiac had inexplicably released into him the glandular dream-life of a twenty-year-old convict with sideburns and a pectoral tattoo showing the genitalia of an Arabian stallion. I press my case only a little. No doubt his medication was having its way again. But this time horniness had supplanted excessive depression and brought him out of the wings as more than a bit player. He said things he probably shouldn't have, and surrendered at times to a harmless but licentious abandon with orderlies and acquaintances. He began to allude to the size of his cock, which he was vain about, and his hand would nestle in his lap. "I have a voracious sexual appetite," he boasted. "I'm proud of my prick." In a house of ageing veterans, some of them gaga, it was a remarkable performance. In more subdued moments he might remember he couldn't really get it up, and, even if he could, a prostate operation years before had left him with no semen to ejaculate.

There was more. He wanted me to know he was "well hung" and that he used to like to offer himself "then take it away" from washroom cocksuckers he didn't like the look of. Did this give him a sense of power? "Power, yes. I could control it." He added, "I like the rough stuff myself." This Ortonesque revelation, and others, seemed like a determined dismantling of the false front of his past life and even of his art. The sexual hypocrisy of marriages he had written about no longer seemed the sort of marriages he would consider writing about in future, were he still able to write fiction. Now he was writing autobiography — or at least relating autobiography, to a fellow writer whom he would like to impress enough (as I imagined it) for him to take note.

I heard about cinemas in Athens, Barcelona, Madrid, Malaga, Mexico City: where you went to have the bulge in your pants assessed and run over with fingers, by "those who liked to do" as opposed to "those who liked to have it done." He said: "I liked to have it done. I never liked to do it." To "do" . . .

this reminded me of the novel he'd written briefly to me about in 1981, about a father and son, which he was to describe again in more (homosexual) detail around this time, calling it, I believe, *Teddy Do.* Oral sex fascinated him. He wanted his "big one" admired. He would repeat that he thought "normal" men "enjoyed it too" — meaning oral sex. "Normal people like to have it done." Wasn't he normal? I asked him. He smiled. "No." He didn't think so.

In his most outrageous stage, his fantasies about having "had" a particular orderly "last night" made it seem he *wasn't* normal, forgetting of course the indelible reality of dreams. His confusion of dreams and reality often seemed so obvious at this time I let it go and waited for the conversation to regain its customary currency of balance and perspective. Dreams were the gremlins. His body knew more than his mind. I would think back to his obsession over not making noise and decide making whoopee was at least preferable. We might go on to discuss a book or trees. But not with the same fervency, for him.

It sometimes seemed as if what he told me — that "it was a long time before I held a male body" — was in some way responsible for his indiscriminate baring of a past he'd like to be remembered by, rather than by the chaste past before that. In 1988, even before these personal revelations began, he'd grown increasingly outspoken about the love that hadn't bothered to speak its name till recently. Whereas earlier it had been, "There's a lot of it around" — meaning homosexuality, with that calculated naïveté he sometimes showed in mentioning a subject that interested him (but one about which he remained happy to repeat received and wishful speculation concerning, say, Canadian hockey players and Spanish bullfighters) — that pitch now became, "I think it started to come out with the invention of the shower." And he'd go on: "It used to be such a messy affair, having anal intercourse, you couldn't imagine going down on someone afterwards."

A couple of days after his first revelations to me about his personal past, I finished reading Lehmann's book and decided one or two passages had possibly prompted him to speak out. As Lehmann writes about Isherwood: "He showed me parts of the new book, which indicated that he was going to make no bones about queerness. I thought it read excellently, and my appetite was much whetted." And (same year): "This time, too, he talked of what he planned to write: it seems that he is engaged in the long work of revising and expanding the diaries he had kept since arriving in the U.S. all that time ago, particularly filling in details of sexual encounters — which he said returned to his memory extremely vividly as soon as he found the notes in his diary. . . ."

I began to suspect that perhaps my friend had recalled from years before a remark my wife had made around our dinner table. In passing conversation about memory she'd mentioned I kept a diary. It was the sort of thing a careful man like Jim would remember. (I think he sometimes worried that as a fiction writer I was a threat to "write him up" in the way, say, Paul Theroux had done Graham Greene in *Picture Palace*, a novel Jim hated.) Now in full-blown autobiographical mood, he might well have decided it was high time to fill in some of his own details of sexual encounters à la Isherwood — but like a cuckoo using another nest, to perpetuate his memory in my diary. It amused me to consider this because he seemed so earnest that I know all about his intimate life.

Maybe I was to play Lehmann to his Isherwood. Perhaps even Mrs. Bentley so he might reinvent Philip. He had sometimes said he'd like to write a novel from Philip's point of view, and if his novel *Teddy Do* (in some ways that novel) had been thrown away in disgust, maybe his diarizing in *my* diary was another way of getting at the truth. I don't know. Certainly Philip needed reinventing, if only to bring him out from behind what I'd long thought of as that novel's ultimate false front.

One speculated at the time concerning his motivation in suddenly divulging so much. From the start of his revelations I even wondered if he wasn't possibly making them all up — using me to discredit his past, to shed scurrilous light on him posthumously — so the future might judge him less a Puritan than it might otherwise be inclined to. It did amuse me to think of him as a character I was writing, indeed a character he was writing, making up the past he hoped would give him the kind of transgressive, raunchy life he felt he'd largely missed out on by not having held that "male body" till so late. Was he daring me to find him out — should he happen to slip up on details when he repeated himself, as he often did?

I was patient. Steam baths in Montreal, a night of debauch by the Thames, a cleric in Westminster, a near-miss with the police in a Madrid (or was it a Barcelona?) cinema. This was a boastful side of him I hardly knew. I expected him to slip — I think I wanted him to slip — in order to increase my admiration for his fictional imagination. Indeed his story of having seven or eight men on a single visit to the Montreal baths left him distinctly vulnerable to such admiration. Yet he was honest: "I didn't come seven or eight times. They liked anybody with a big one." In spite of the failing memory that worried him increasingly over the years, he never slipped up in repeating these intimate revelations to me. It seemed a kind of memory test for him, a way of shaping and reshaping his life. He was, like Philip, consistent in a repetitive kind of way. He got rather tedious, frankly. I do think he knew what he was up to and was determined to tell me the truth. In lieu of a love life, he did want it known that he'd had a sex life.

I knew he hadn't exaggerated what he was proudest of — the size of his penis — because I'd accidentally glimpsed it a few years before under the loose gown he wore when he was removed from his apartment to have a pin put in his hip. I was helping him down the hospital corridor to the toilet. I suppose his pride in having "a big one" was his way of surmounting a small man's physical insecurity, even shame for his perceived sissy youth. Perhaps his cock was the means by which he'd always hoped to attract the "long lean" body he confessed was his ideal man (and not coincidentally the repetitive figure of several of his male protagonists, including Philip in his first novel, Coulter in "Jug and Bottle," Spike in "Spike," and the sex-murderer father in "The Flowers That Killed Him" — each of whom is precisely six feet three inches tall). I am inclined to think his largely unspoken obsession with his own missing father (tall and good-looking, according to Jim) whom he never saw again after age nine, was responsible for a pattern of thinking about the men he identified with for the rest of his adult life. But of course the image of these men with their long skinny necks and hunched shoulders, not to mention their "puniness" as children, was also the image he retained of himself.

It wasn't until a couple of years after the increasingly intimate revelations about himself began, that he came back to the notion of whether *As for Me and My House* might in fact be a homoerotic book. Perhaps I should have pressed him earlier, out of sheer curiosity about his own thinking on what seemed to me an obvious theme, but I thought if he was suspicious in some way about my loyalty to what he was understandably jealous of, his art, it was best to let him come back to this topic on his own. Four years after first bringing up the question, he did finally acknowledge the homosexuality in his novel in the bathetic, but significant, comment: "It's there." He wanted me to know it was there, but "unintentional."

It had thus taken him eight years (with me) to acknowledge what he never had before. Yet first he'd had to narrate past conquests by relating these as he might have visits to the opera complete with plot summary and melodrama. "I like melodrama," he'd said years earlier in Athens. He was coming to an understanding of how his homosexuality, despite a false front, might be present in his most famous novel without his necessarily having detected it himself, in what he assumed was a carefully constructed marriage *in extremis*. One recalls that earlier observation: "I suppose a man would write that way whether he knew he was one or not." He knew, but was writing otherwise.

Critics have alluded to the mythopoeic qualities of this classic novel of a loveless marriage, and these are no doubt present in the story's haunting portrait of elements and landscape, in the stripping down of human emotions between a husband and wife. Yet I also think of it as a soap opera with adultery, bastards, jealousies, and small-town gossip. It is, in other words, a story you read for both poetry and narrative, a novel simultaneously dramatic and lyrical.

Rereading it within a week of the author's death, on a trip through India and Sri Lanka, I was surprised at how vivid the writing remained after half a century, the scenes etched deeply in arias of place and circumstance. There's a deep and practical intelligence at work, generating pawky language and laconic rhythms. I was struck by how the *sound* of this language transcends the time of its writing, and how this achievement of voice happens elsewhere in his work so rarely (especially when dialogue in a later novel like *Whir of Gold* sounds like a dated movie script). I marvelled at how evocative his voice still was of dust and ennui through which I myself was now struggling to make my way in very different surroundings of "dense, sickly heat." I could remember writing from Bombay to Ross, then in Spain, twenty-three years earlier to the week, and felt a circle like Mrs. Bentley's "wide wheel" now closing as I came to the end of his book.

In reopening it now, I feel burdened with the knowledge that it's so *much* about its author, so personally allusive, that any attempt to read it the way I believe it needs to be read will make it seem far more complex than it appears on the surface to be. I suppose this can only enhance its status as an inexhaustible text, despite any irreverence shown it. More than almost any other Canadian novel one might name, it's a solipsistic novel disguised with characters.

One concludes it is all about the way "Sinclair Ross" divided himself. (Sinclair was his middle name, but he had adopted it as his pen name because it sounded more worldly than James or Jimmy. Something about that "Sin" would have tickled him, not to mention the French allusion to the "clarity" of his style.) Whatever seed planted this story in his mind (evidently a minister he knew, his dying wife, and a housekeeper), the world of the novel suggests it drew directly on his own intimate history: on living closely with his mother, on not living with his father; on his view of marriage based on his parents' rift; on his sense of and infatuation with the dispossessed, even dead, child he felt himself to be; on his particular interests in painting, etymology, piano; on the back-biting small-town environments he'd survived as a young man; on his familiarity with the Church as an organist and with what he once passed up in not agreeing to become a minister like Philip (who sells his soul to marriage and the devil); and on his prophetic sense of public failure as an artist, even as he was writing his novel.

But mainly what I want to suggest is how the author's divided self is also present in a homoerotic way and how this contributes to a flaw in the novel that is forced to pretend such a self isn't present. This particular false front of Philip's is glimpsed but not admitted as are his other selves of hypocritical minister, resentful husband, and closet artist. These are all housed in the same body and fronted by a loveless marriage.

3

At supper one night soon after coming to Vancouver, Ross said the only time he could distinctly remember writing *As for Me and My House* was during a two-week summer vacation in a cottage he rented with "another boy" on Lake Winnipeg. They were there in 1939 when the phoney war began in September. He didn't say what part of the novel he'd reached, though it was less than half way through, he said. His usual pattern of writing his book, when he was working full-time at the bank, was an hour or two on the side, in the evenings and on weekends in Winnipeg. Earlier in Athens he'd remembered how it took him two years writing in longhand, and then, rereading it, how he thought it was awful. He typed the manuscript and retyped it, "tightening the texture, if you know what I mean." He was living with his mother then, writing of an earlier period in Saskatchewan when, not incidentally, he'd also been living with his mother and in a small town not unlike Horizon of the novel. (Abbey, not Arcola, he said, was closer to Horizon. But what is much more interesting to note is that because Jim and his mother left Saskatchewan for Winnipeg when he was in his mid-twenties, the prime material of most of his stories and novels derives from an early age.

Little he'd go on to write of his later adult life, in Montreal, say, would ring as true.)

He once explained to me that his mother used to cover up for the fact her son didn't seem interested in girls by telling outsiders: "No girl is good enough for him," or, "Oh, he's an artist." (Maybe this was why Jim hated the term "artist," because of his mother's mocking association of it with someone superior or odd.) Mrs. Bentley uses the same excuse on more than one occasion. "It's the artist in him" is how she puts it in her diary by way of excusing her husband's predispositions. "In Philip's likes and dislikes there's always something troubled and smoldering."* My own sense is that Mrs. Bentley doesn't really want to know what that "something" is — even when she knows it. "The doctor insists it's environment, not heredity, so when you hear what I've been hearing simply shut your ears" (79), Mrs. Bird, the doctor's wife, abruptly and rather oddly tells her around the time of their taking in the adolescent Steve. Shutting her ears, her eyes . . . Mrs. Bentley (you think) is not unlike the novelist himself here (indeed she *is* the novelist himself here), reluctant to acknowledge what is staring them in the face, or to more than hint at it out of a repressed social anxiety.

---

* Sinclair Ross, *As for Me and My House*, New Canadian Library 4 (Toronto: McClelland, 1957; reprinted 1989) 168. All further references in the text are to this edition. Incidentally, I wish the New Canadian Library could see fit to invest some of its profits from this novel in a new edition, devoted to correcting the typos it has perpetuated since republishing the 1941 edition.

Not so thirty-three years later in *Sawbones Memorial* (1974), when the bit player Benny Fox acknowledges Doc Hunter's kind advice in liberating his thinking about himself as a young homosexual of twenty in the small town of Upward. This novel was Ross's unexpected fourth — unexpected more for its form and quality, after two preceding failures, than for any revelation about its author. Yet this novel, unlike his first, is explicit rather than implicit in its sexual revelation. I daresay living with a mother had had its convenient false front of protection for a gay son, even when "she," in Benny's view, had contributed to his present condition by dressing him in effeminate clothes as a child and in general by exacerbating his feelings of persecution. If this homosexual piano player is anything to go by, town gossip about Ross as a young man — and what "environmental" damage his mother might have done him — wasn't just fictionalizing on his part. "Well, she and Sam were certainly normal enough — at least judging by the fix they got themselves into — so he didn't inherit it," gossips one of Upward's women. And the other woman jokes about this kind of man: "I know they like each other instead of us, but just what is it exactly that they *do*?"* Ross told me once how his mother had quizzed him after his return from a picnic with his piano teacher, Frank Woodbury, because "the whole town was talking." He and Frank, a reputed

---

* Sinclair Ross, *Sawbones Memorial,* New Canadian Library 145 (Toronto: McClelland, 1978) 49.

pedophile, used to pal around. ("Well, I don't know *exactly* what they do, Rose, but stop and think a minute how they're made. What *can* they do?") That Frank was "effeminate" suggests another model for Benny Fox besides Jimmy Ross, though the biographical details favour the author for this (perhaps composite) character. (Frank, he let me know, was envious of his early writing and never mentioned it. And because Jim had developed into a better pianist than his teacher, other students wanted to take lessons from him instead.)

The sort of relaxed perspective in the later novel is severely limited and not very clear in the earlier and more important one. Restricted to Mrs. Bentley's point of view, what we, the voyeurs of her diary, learn is shuttered and claustrophobic, incestuous and unadmitted. "Philip, Steve and I. It's such a trim, efficient little sign; it's such a tough, deep-rooted tangle that it hides." She goes on: "And none of them knows. They spy and carp and preen themselves, but none of them knows" (81). In reading this, you feel the religious hypocrisy of an artistic-leaning preacher only goes so far in explaining what "none of them knows."

There's also the unacknowledged hypocrisy to do with Philip's longing for a boy. "An unwanted, derided little outcast, exactly what he used to be himself" (70). The double image of Philip becomes increasingly narcissistic as the novel unfolds. Lacking self love he seems obsessed with finding it. "He likes boys — often, I think, plans the bringing-up and education of *his* boy" (9). That his wife is

48

sterile and he wants a son isn't at all, you feel, why Philip welcomes the "ominously good-looking" Steve. Steve begins to sound like a mountable fantasy for him. "Philip has taken him for Pegasus, and gone off to the clouds again" (70). Her husband is besotted by this boy — or, as Mrs. Bentley would have it, his "dream" of this boy.

It's a kind of wish-fulfilment dream for Philip to have Steve in the same house with his wife's connivance, planning his bedroom, taking him alone for car rides, dressing him up, buying him treats and a pony. Ponies, horseplay, mannish women, trunkless men, stovepipes, tobacco pipes, Hereford bulls, hands on shoulders . . . "It's there," as Ross eventually acknowledged . . . the unspoken love of an older man for a younger one, even in extraneous sexual clues that go both ways. I happen to know that later on in his life Jim also adopted a boy, far from Saskatchewan, and that his experience which began ideally like Philip's ended abruptly. His character's longing is subliminal. Just as his wife's remains mostly subliminal, as in this sentence you swear is lifted from an early page of *The Great Gatsby*: "For like draws to like, they say, which makes it reasonable to suppose that, when you've just walked away from a man because you feel he doesn't want to be bothered with you, you're capable of attracting a few ghouls and demons anyway" (126). (Only the word "anyway" gives it a characteristic Ross touch — "enniweh" as he would pronounce it in a clipped prairie way.)

And so rereading his novel we are challenged to "read the signals," as Benny puts it to Doc Hunter at the advanced (sexual) age of thirty-two. This age, interestingly, was a year younger than Ross was when he published *As for Me and My House*. Benny still lives in Horizon, stuck there "with the tar pot and pillows" always a threat — but Jim had escaped. The trouble is, by not giving voice to Benny's story for *another* thirty-three years, the author failed to devise a strategy for dealing successfully with his own "queerness" in earlier works. He paid an artistic price for his timidity which Isherwood, as he recognized, had avoided from the start in a more cosmopolitan climate. For it was his earliest critic who detected something fundamentally the matter with his plot.

Jim told me his mother's only observation about the book was this: "She wouldn't have stayed. She'd have left him." It was Mrs. Bentley's "devotion," he said in Athens, his mother had questioned. I must confess to favouring Mrs. Ross's criticism of Mrs. Bentley. This is really it in a nutshell, though a lot of nuts have been shelled looking for something else to explain the enigma in the novel — in short, that "she's too good to be true; too self-deceiving to be believed." For his mother it was a simple matter of credibility. It seems surprising no one since has spoken out in such practical terms.

Mrs. Bentley, a sharp independent-minded woman, debases herself for a man who treats her abominably. She *is* too good to be true — if doggish loyalty is considered good. Yet the author thinks we're given enough of a look behind Philip's facade to see why his wife would want to stay with a basically good and decent man. Ross always stuck up for Philip (as he did his father) and would tell fans that Philip is such a sour and aloof character only because of his honest awareness of himself as a hypocrite. But how far does this self-awareness really go?

The problem goes back to the origins of the novel. Jim often explained how he began it as Philip's book and then "she" took over. "I like Philip, but people who read my book generally don't," he admitted many years ago, watching male Greek dancers breaking dishes on a restaurant floor in the Plaka. Later when the articles started in on the untrustworthiness of his narrator, and gained in fashionable consensus over the years, thereby placing the inchoate Philip in a better light than was apparent in the book, he eventually went along with these essays and came to see how what he never intended by way of a scheming narrator could be used to exonerate his own defence of Philip, and — I think as a bonus — to contradict his mother's criticism that his plot didn't add up when Mrs. Bentley insists on standing by her man.

"She was a bookish woman," he'd told me in Athens. "The Scots, you know, have a great respect for learning." He was talking about his mother. Her criticism of his novel must have given him pause, no matter how jealous and dismissive she'd been of his writing. She, after all, had left *her* husband and knew what she was talking about as an independent-minded woman with probably less aplomb — less "ear" for discord — than the musical Mrs. Bentley. My suspicion is Mrs. Bentley was a kind of anti–Mrs. Ross. You got the feeling he never forgave his mother for leaving his father and that his novel in some way was a sublimation of his wish that she'd tried harder to keep the family together. (It didn't matter that she *had* tried, twice.) Jim's gradual agreement over the years with critics who saw more and more duplicity in Mrs. Bentley was in effect a way of distancing himself from, indeed denying, his mother's criticism of his novel. And paradoxically the more the "good" Mrs. Bentley receded into a kind of "bad" Mrs. Bentley, the closer she got to Mrs. Ross. This would have been a nice revenge. Their house was too small for an artist as well as a critic.

The guilt and self-contempt Ross was willing to acknowledge in his protagonist had of course to do with Philip's religious — not his sexual — hypocrisy. While this is where the novel derives its considerable metaphysical force, if that's the word for how it fronts nature's whirling indifference in Mrs. Bentley's descants, at the same time it feels incomplete on a physical level. You could argue this is the point of the story. Yet at what point does incomplete become inconsistent, dramatically speaking? You get the sense an awful lot of the resentment Philip feels towards his wife stems from his frustrated sexuality and not from his religious doubt.

Try substituting the *one* false front for the other in this sentence: "In our lives it isn't the Church [*marriage*] itself that matters but what he feels about it, the shame and sense of guilt he suffers while remaining a part of it. That's why we're adopting Judith's baby. He'll not dare let his son see him as he sees himself; and he's no dissembler" (203). But her husband is a dissembler and Mrs. Bentley knows it. They're even in cahoots when it comes to dissembling. The pair of them shares his religious hypocrisy. She also admires his closeted art. So you do feel, with this empathy of hers for his false position as a preacher, with this support and unending patience of hers for his incarceration as an artist, that there has to be some other reason for the quite shitty way he reacts to and treats her. I'm suggesting he hates his marriage as much as he does the Church for imprisoning him behind a false front.

But by failing to make the homoerotic imagery *matter* with respect to the plot, by failing even to acknowledge its existence except in ambiguous ways, Mrs. Bentley and the author misread Philip's character and misjudge her own. They hope to persuade us to read Philip as being flawed in an aesthetically *acceptable* way, when the reverse is true. His false front is even more tangled than they're able to admit. This leads to a dramatically unsatisfying resolution, a kind of syrupy dénouement. In this way, notwithstanding his considerable accomplishment, Ross curried at the end more artifice than art. Even he thought his novel was deficient and wished to rewrite the ending by keeping Judith West alive and her baby from the Bentleys. (He told me he wished to give this novel the rather monographic title *If Judith Were Different*.) Where would this have landed the seemingly reinvigorated marriage of the Bentleys? Where it belonged, Mrs. Ross would have said, on the rocks. The last part of the novel had given him the most trouble, and he felt he'd taken the easy way out.

By not admitting Philip's homosexuality in the novel, so it might have made a difference to the drama or effected a less stilted outcome, Ross compromised the credibility of his main heterosexual relationship. Philip is flawed, not in the acceptable literary sense of a character's flaw out of which the story flows (Hamlet, Lear); but in the sense of an artistic flaw out of which the story fails to flow but ought to. Emotionally, the novel fails to evolve the way its "signals" suggest it might have if the truth of Philip's nature were voiced and his last real hypocrisy dealt with.

It isn't that Mrs. Bentley *chooses* to ignore his nature — which might have added even more to the novel's power, as a book transcendent of bigoted attitudes in its time and place — she simply doesn't see her husband in a way that affords her the choice. What she *does* see is a future of his continuing indifference to her, with her thinking she can win back his love. "[D]eep inside I know that a thousand dollars and getting away from Horizon isn't nearly so important as I'm pretending to believe. Not so far as I'm concerned, anyway. It will make him think more of himself maybe, but it won't make him think any more of me. Deep inside I even know that it really isn't Judith. She was just there. Another time somebody else will be there" (171). In effect she agrees to continue as his doormat when what "her" house requires is leaving it.

So how exactly does the novel end up in this predicament that has caused such erudite argument in its defence? In a court of criticism I would probably begin by trying to show how what Mrs. Bentley calls "dramatically right" (74) — in Judith's own decision to walk out on the man who wants to marry her — can be differentiated from what we might call "morally right," which is what concerns the gossips in town regarding Judith, the Bentleys, and Steve. *They* don't give a fig for what's *dramatically* right, because that way lies risk, subversion, even art such as Philip's — threats to the homogeneous norm. What seems morally right to these bigots is that as a Catholic Steve has no place in a Protestant house. They force him to leave. Mrs. Bentley on the other hand does not leave, although it might seem dramatically right for her to have done something of the sort. You get the inescapable sense that the drama in this novel, honed to reveal how love between a minister and his wife has been corrupted, is subtly skewed in favour of what is "morally right."

What isn't dramatically right is that a smart, determined, self-reliant Mrs. Bentley is pathetically dependent on the non-love of a stolid, unlikeable man who bitterly resents her, tries to replace her with Steve, commits adultery with Judith, and shuts her out of his life whenever he can. Why does she debase herself time and again, and furthermore, not only stick by her misogynist husband in the end but offer happily to take in his bastard infant? Why in spite of her strength of mind and purpose is she such a doormat? Is it because, as now a herd of critics has suggested, she is stage-managing events and him to her own ends? Is it because she really isn't telling us the truth about her motives in her diary? These sorts of arguments have proliferated over the years in order, I suggest, to redeem what "doesn't add up" in the novel (to repeat one of Ross-the-bank-clerk's favourite expressions) — thereby exonerating its weakness centred in one's instinctive dislike of Philip, and to promote the novel as an even better book than it is by touting the ironic ambiguity of Mrs. Bentley's supposedly unlikeable character.

Perhaps her peculiar behaviour derives from a failure to admit or want to know what her husband's sexuality really is. "And in the darkness perhaps I see clearly — but I don't admit it. Don't dare admit it" (99). This complicity with the author allows Ross to have it both ways, an artistic failing. Apparently, neither he nor we really notice what Mrs. Bentley tells us: "Women weren't necessary or important to him as to most men" (22). This she's recognized from the start of their courtship. And now a dozen years later: "Comfort and routine were the last things he needed. Instead he ought to have been out mingling with his own kind. He ought to have whetted himself against them, then gone off to fight it out alone. He ought to have had the opportunity to live, to be reckless, spendthrift, bawdy, anything but what he is, what I've made him" (135–36). Another environmental argument? She sounds like a mother burdened with a housebound "queer" à la Benny Fox. No, she certainly doesn't want to stay with Philip for the sex, nor for his thoughtful conversations, nor for his jealousies, nor for his adultery now or in the future. So why? Because she believes in him? Pities him? Owes him a son for having a miscarriage? Thinks she can persuade him to love her like a normal man? Because she's on a power trip? Any way you compute it, it hardly adds up.

It can only be because, deep down and fundamentally, the novelist thought more of Philip than the reader does, and his narrator feels obliged to comport herself accordingly. Ross felt his artist figure in Philip to be sympathetic and heroic (a kind of self-portrait whose youthful "sidle" and "puniness" and bastardish background matched his). This wilful blindness becomes his narrator's. She knows her husband *so* well — how he breathes when he isn't asleep, what he's thinking, his jealousy over Steve — that she knows she doesn't know him intimately at all. This is especially evident in the desolate bedroom scenes when intimacy is denied her. Thus about Philip's unadmitted sexuality you come to conclude that the book knows more than either she *or* the author knows — just as the body often knows more than the mind.

Mrs. Bentley takes understandable comfort in her recurrent belief that Judith means nothing to her philandering spouse. Yet she explains his behaviour as arising from his grieving for Steve's departure. "I've been right all the time. It really isn't Judith. He was trying to escape that night, trying to prove to himself that Steve after all didn't matter. And she just happened to be there" (167). This is odd consolation you think for his losing a *son*. Is she obsessed with Judith, or is it really Steve, at the root of her obsession? "And his passion for Steve, dark, strange and morbid passion that it was, accounting for that is the tangle of his early years, dark, strange, and morbid most of them too" (177). The language itself comes increasingly to mirror Philip's identity, while her own identity is reflected doggishly in his. "I'm help-less and weak and spiritless before him. There's nothing left inside me but a panting animal. . . . The way I watch his face for a flicker of awareness or desire . . ." (199).

She seems bound to her husband by some instinct deeper than thought. That his sexual and emotional nature is unresponsive to hers, except in a mechan-ical way, doesn't appear to surprise her although it shames her. She has accepted her marriage as a false front (166). In the town's terms her hypocrisy in this acceptance would be considered morally right. But not, you feel, in her own terms dramatically inevit-able. You are tempted to conclude that the gulf between her independent spirit and her decision to go on trying to please Philip owes much to the fear and social expectations, indeed the false front, Ross himself had continued to live behind with his mother.

(When he finally left his mother and enlisted in the Canadian Army in 1942, one feels it was the great event of his life because he'd found the morally *and* dramatically right thing for himself in offering to serve his country. That this was another false front for him, living incognito in the sudden proximity of countless men, could only have increased his ironic sense that no matter how many facades you peeled back life was shadowed by a duality — sometimes a contrived duality — that would continue to haunt his fiction in the war novel he destroyed.)

One of the novel's first reviewers in the spring of 1941 was Robertson Davies, who, unlike the earliest reviewer, found "the relationship between the husband and wife . . . though complex and perverse . . . entirely credible. Finally, the chief theme of the book is a love affair that went wrong, and here . . . Mr. Ross has been able to treat a sexual theme with restraint, so that although his picture is complete it never becomes dirty." Well no, actually. One is certainly willing to concede "restraint" — but feels there's an *in*completeness about this "perverse" picture precisely because it *doesn't* become "dirty."

There was something stunted in the way Ross viewed sexual relations of either persuasion, and I'll come back to his notions of love. But certainly, flattering the male vanity characterizes the sex, or lack of it, in his fiction. That and a sometimes cruel or violent undercurrent. Yet dominance and submission, as between Philip and his wife, or between Philip and Judith, gives way before a kind of ideal homoerotic love you detect in Philip's attraction to his adopted son. The lack of any "dirtiness" makes it harder to detect, and harder to account for it when you do.

His possessive (and repetitive) hands on Steve's shoulders, as Jim told me, "is a very homosexual gesture." ("I knew it was when I wrote it," he asserted, contradicting a later claim. But I wonder if he did know it. It would have diminished him as an artist, knowing this and having done nothing to develop it in the novel.) Also homosexual, in varying degrees, is Philip's staring and staring at the boy —

repeated later in his looking and looking at his infant son — his patent jealousy over Steve, his desire to shut out his wife and have the boy to himself. "It's only since we've had Steve with us that I've realized how much of himself a man has to give before he's really possessed" (144), Mrs. Bentley confides to her diary. What emerges is a spreading suggestiveness apparent once you turn the sexual key in Philip's door. "Why can't you take hold and do things like other men?" (175) asks his loveless wife. One *wants* this suggestiveness to bear the weight of metaphorical meaning. One wants the stovepipes he can't handle around *her* to link up with the firehose he takes charge of among men at the town fire. One wants, in other words, an accountable author, for whom things "add up." Yet this suggestiveness never takes its dramatic responsibility seriously. The novel on one level is a wet dream.

The earlier short stories had often been about loveless, passionless marriages. Then enters in the novel this kind of love, ideal and homoerotic, which seems to carry on what crops up in a story preceding the novel, "Cornet at Night." One notes the Fitzgeraldish rhythms: "I wanted to know what it felt like to take young men with yellow shoes in my stride, to be preoccupied, to forget them the moment we separated. And I did."* This disinterest in emotional attachment is revealing, I think, for it tends to

---

* Sinclair Ross, *The Lamp at Noon and Other Stories*, New Canadian Library 62 (Toronto: McClelland, 1968) 38.

rationalize a pride Ross felt in his own ability to shed baggage when it threatened his independence. He didn't seem to need people the way most people did. He didn't need women the way most men did. He was usually the outsider, looking for excuses not to be invited in. As Mrs. Bentley writes of her husband: "He was forever being disillusioned, forever finding people out and withdrawing into himself with a sense of hurt and grievance" (44). Yet in her it seemed Ross was hedging his bet, keeping her close: "An idol turned clay can make even an earthly woman desirable" (157). She goes on trying to convince herself that nature will win out, when it's nature that's the problem neither she nor the author will admit.

Although Philip's disillusionment with Steve begins subtly to appear when Steve ends up aboard the mare Minnie, rather than the young Pegasus-like sorrel, you notice that, with the boy's early departure from their home, the older man's ideal love for him manages to transcend what's been "perverted, and its better nature lost." This is how the novel talks about straight love, about words that "while [they] socially come up in the world, most of them morally go down." Mrs. Bentley learns from Paul Kirby, how "Cupid . . . has given us *cupidity*, Eros, *erotic*, Venus, *venereal*, and Aphrodite, *aphrodisiac*" (101). You almost pause for him to add, in his knowledgeable way, how homo has given us (after 1897) *homosexual*. But of course this one still had yet to "come up socially in the world" at the time when Ross was writing between the wars. It was only the rare writer, like Isherwood, who didn't "apologize" for his bent.

So what does one make of all this? Perhaps that Mrs. Bentley's voice had got away on him, gloriously, creating its own rather independent character which then went against what the author felt committed to impose on her: a kind of traditional moral acceptance of her husband, for better or for worse, because he (the author) continued to believe in Philip as better than he reads. "Sometimes you've simply got to be hard," writes Mrs. Bentley of her relentless pursuit of towns owing back payments to her husband. "Nobody thinks any more of you for keeping quiet and taking what they offer" (165). A lot of *readers* haven't thought more of her for keeping quiet and taking what she's offered — her husband's child by another woman. Critics on the other hand have come up with all sorts of gossip to show how she gets not only what she wants but has coming to her. My own feeling, however, is the author has given her the dirty end of the stick.

The novel's last line is extremely revealing of the dramatic flaw I see in the novel's plot. It's the paradox of the plot that Mrs. Bentley *does* "keep quiet" about what she really feels. For when she replies silently to her husband in this line — "That's right, Philip. I want it so" — you might be forgiven for thinking it sounds a little more like the author wanting it so than his long-suffering character. Her "better" is now bonded forever to Philip's "worse."

This well-known last line refers to Philip's self-satisfied concern that by naming his son Philip his wife will get the two of them mixed up and "won't know which of us is which." This ending strikes me as facile, self-regarding, and even incestuous. It reflects not only Philip's vanity but the author's. The complex relationship of Philip and son is intended to mirror his past, I think, to reflect his abiding feelings of loss as a bastard himself, to see in it his stillborn son and dead preacher father, not to mention a consolation of sorts for losing Steve, his adopted son, and possibly even to show off the infant as a sort of heterosexual trophy. The pattern-making is pronounced. So is the artifice. The business of the name reflects the author's own satisfaction at having brought off Philip, I would suggest, in his own image.

At the end of the novel Paul Kirby tells Mrs. Bentley that her choice of names for the baby is an adroit one: " 'It means a lover* of horses,' he said. 'You couldn't get a better one.' " Indeed not — though the reader might be forgiven for wondering *why* not, apart from all the other horseplay in the story in which Philip plays his shadowy part. For if you take this naming to its truly narcissistic conclusion, the author's name — Ross — means "horse" (which he pointed out to me more than once when we'd talk about names and words in the English Bay Cafe, or else in some tacky Chinese restaurant along Denman Street).

If Philip *is* a lover of horses, it's obvious where this character's affections coyly lie. And his creator has reciprocated these by favouring his offstage

---

* This word "lover," from the original 1941 edition has inexplicably lost its "r" in the New Canadian Library edition.

protagonist over his onstage antagonist with everything he wants — including his freedom, a city bookstore, and a boy. (This mirrors the way Philip favours Steve with everything *he* wants, until Steve exits the story.) The upbeat ending, full of wishes fulfilled, feels more morally correct than dramatically right. It plays to the town, to the Main Street Philip has drawn with its false fronts: "[T]hey stare at each other across the street as into mirrors of themselves, absorbed in their own reflections" (91). It's a glassy finale. "He doesn't look like Philip yet, but Philip I'll swear is starting to look like him" (216). Ross has become both Philips in a penstroke. (And he even finds the family and community that has eluded him as an orphan, an outsider, and a timid homosexual.) Quite a houseful of mirrors, and not stretching it by much. I know of no other Canadian novel in which the self of the author is quite so completely the centre of attention.

But at what cost? Mrs. Bentley: "For a long time he held aloof. At heart, I think, he was distrustful not only of me but all my kind. It was friendship he wanted, someone to realize in flesh and blood the hero-worship that he had clung to all through his hard adolescence. He would just half-yield himself to me, then stand detached, self-sufficient. It was as if this impulse to seek me out made him feel guilty, as if he felt he were being false to himself. Perhaps, too, he knew instinctively that as a woman I would make claims upon him, and that as an artist he needed above all things to be free" (44). I think if you substitute "homosexual" for "artist" — an interchangeableness Rilke might have encouraged in the little book *Letters to a Young Poet* Jim received on his last birthday — you can see what the author had made plainer than he knew about his protagonist. His wife knows what her husband doesn't, and what the novelist won't let her act on. She knows and she doesn't know; the novel knows and it wants us to ask. "The books understand, but you don't," she writes of Philip's library and herself. "It's always loyal to him. It sees and knows him for what he really is, but it won't let slip a word" (61).

No reading can be definitive, only convincing. And persuasion is a moveable art. One is drawn into this mirrory book out of a memoirist's vanity, wondering if it's fooling you the way it has others. So much of its meaning you feel lies in the frame of the novel. But which frame? It has tricked critics into believing its story lies in the narrator rather than in the narrator of its narrator. (It is *he* who is unreliable.) But this is heretical. Biography is supposed to complement, not define, the body of a work. And a memoir's no place to parade one's ignorance of French theoretical fashion. Yet the commentary surrounding this landmark novel has risked frustration by excluding its author as a *character*. For you eventually come to the conclusion that "Sinclair Ross" is the shadow character, staring and staring like Philip, *at* Philip, and without whom the novel can't be fully understood.

Because of his reluctance to give interviews or to be a public person, the idea and extent of Ross's solipsistic fiction has never emerged. The unevenness of his books and the rural remoteness of his good ones — at either end of a long career — have conspired to limit his interest for us. But he *is* an interesting writer. You would have thought his false fronts and dual imaginings, his sometimes contrived pattern-seeking to justify melodramatic plots, his obsession with identity and how this limits — and doesn't limit — empathy, along with his compulsion to withhold characters from emotional commitment, would be quite conducive to postmodernist theories of self, and I foresee a new wave of attention for Jim Ross's writings in the new century.

I hope they remember the man.

4

Ross had understood at a very young age you can make art of your own world. This was ahead of its time in Canada, let alone rural Canada. And he proceeded to address himself to what art is, with a boldness that later startled him. He couldn't believe he'd had "the nerve" to write that way, or got the novel so well in parts. Art that copied art was not art. It was prose, such as what Philip tries on occasion to write. But art that learned from art, commented on art, discussed itself as this novel slyly does, was genuine. It had an immediate appeal for young Canadian intellectuals like Northrop Frye.

He was an academic at the University of Toronto when Ross met him in 1941, at a luncheon attended by Robertson Davies, Earle Birney, and E.J. Pratt in his honour. Jim said simply he "didn't rise to the occasion." Frye later invited him alone to a gay restaurant for dinner and alluded to the homosexuals at the university. " 'Of course you know what I'm talking about,' " Ross quoted Frye as saying to him. I have no idea whether his dislike of Frye had to do with this assumption on Frye's part, or if his dislike arose from his characteristic feelings of inadequacy around intellectuals and his looking for a reason to be disillusioned. (He took a similar dislike to Birney when they met again in London in 1943. And forty years later, when I arranged to introduce him to George Woodcock over lunch, he was intimidated although affable. I remember he decided *not* to wear a tie. I seem to recall his once telling me a tie or the absence of one had been part of the problem in meeting Birney in uniform. His interest in rank and social appearances was acute.)

Frye on the other hand must have felt an instinctive camaraderie, both with Ross and his novel, given that he himself had been trained like Philip as a minister and spent five wretched months in the summer of 1934 serving the United Church on the Saskatchewan prairie. When Frye died aged seventy-eight, the day after Jim's eighty-third birthday, Jim admitted he'd never read any of his books.

But Frye had read his book. I sometimes feel he owed Mrs. Bentley a debt for stimulating his thinking about the different levels of language he enunciates in, say, *The Educated Imagination*. I would invite readers to turn up Mrs. Bentley's diary entry for July 28, five paragraphs from the end. Am I *wrong* to detect a later echo of Frye here? "Now it's always when a man turns away from this common-sense world around him that he begins to create . . ." (148). Then turn back two or so pages to where Mrs. Bentley is discussing the article Philip is writing for a missionary magazine. She discusses his prose: "well written, all his sentences and paragraphs rounded out sonorously with the puffy, imageless language that gives dignity to church literature, a few well-placed quotations from scripture, and for peroration unbounded faith in the Lord's watchfulness over flocks and shepherds alike" (145). The prose she wittily mirrors here is the linguistic extension of her husband's hypocrisy, the language of the false front hiding his artist's imagination. Something like Frye's second level of language to do with theology perhaps; a bodiless language, compared to the language of literature at the highest level.

Ross had a keen ear for prose. Yet when he wrote "prose" fiction instead of "voice" fiction he produced mediocre work. He could write prose well, but he never wrote any convincing novel in "prose." *The Well* (1958) is an attempt at a third-person novel, which is often full of nuance and nicely modulated sentences, but dead as fiction. What he himself once said (accurately) of another novelist's work might well apply to his own second novel: "His English is beautiful. The characters don't come off the page." We never believe his own characters or care enough about their situations here. Little seems "dramatically right." The insights lack the power of a voice that yearns deeply. It's a complacent voice, his prose voice, a controlling voice of plot not ardour. "He prided himself too much on playing his role well, on being unique in this as in everything else, to begin coldly," he writes of his protagonist's approach to sex with women. "At such times, moreover, there was often a cruel vanity at work, a desire to be remembered and regretted, to cast a blight of inadequacy on whoever might come after him" (131). He knew this novel was a failure and always acknowledged it as such. He even tried to rewrite it. And he wanted to rewrite the novel that followed it a dozen years later, *Whir of Gold*, in which he was trying to get back to "voice" fiction but in which the banality of dialogue is pervasive, unhelped by the narrator's seemingly absent voice.

It's hard to believe now that the voice in the pair of stories he salvaged from his discarded war novel of the mid-forties is from the writer of *As for Me and My House*. I don't think Jim could ever quite understand what had happened to him as a writer in that relatively short span, between composing his first novel at the war's start and his failure to complete a second to his satisfaction after the war. "I knew nothing when I left the prairies, nothing!" he told me in Athens. "And the things I found so new in London, others thought ordinary and banal." You have to think in entering the larger cosmopolitan world of London he took on something of its camouflage in the voices of its authors. And these were the prose voices of Conrad and James. Later, once removed to Montreal from Winnipeg, he somehow lost the obsession of his earlier novel and short stories. He lost his roots. In a way the price of this move was his death as an artist but the birth of a cosmopolitan.

I think he didn't yearn passionately enough in his work after the war to develop as a writer. Perhaps he wasn't temperamentally equipped to develop in the way his promise foreshadowed in his first novel with its astonishingly sophisticated voice, unique and lapidary. You sense that his shyness, his insecurity about himself and body, his homosexuality, family obligation and society's straitjacket, the banker's profession to complement his instinctive caution, the severing of roots: all these inhibited his artistic development. But so did the sophistication (the prose) of the urban environments he went on to visit or to live in as he grew older, the languages he studied on his own until eventually he spoke and read in French, Italian, Greek, Spanish: these conspired to keep him from developing his own voice. My impression on first meeting Jim, in Athens, had been that as a young writer he had written because he had something *instinctive* to say, but then, as a published author, he'd gone on writing because he came to expect it of himself, whether he had anything to say or not.

He felt somehow phoney as a "prose" writer. Prose presupposed knowledge, and he seldom professed to having any, though he read widely his whole life in history and music and literature and art and psychology, hoping to make up for what he felt he'd missed out on by not completing a formal education. Prose wasn't his language, but belonged to the books he read and admired. He felt presumptuous in claiming such language as his own. In an anthology of wartime writing he once gave me (*Transformation*), I see where he has marked several sentences in an article by Stephen Spender, including this one: "They [the English poets between the wars] were attracted by two theories which made a radical diagnosis, the one of the ills of society, the other of the relationship of the individual to society: in the first case, Marxism, in the second, psycho-analysis." Had he been offered membership among these writers whom he once said he'd loved to have known, Jim would have readily joined up in the second camp of Auden and Isherwood. Yet what kind of work would have emerged from an urban Ross?

While written in the first person singular, "Jug and Bottle" (1949) sounds like the work of another writer. Conrad, perhaps, but there are echoes of Ford and Hardy and James. It's fascinating from a biographical point of view to notice how "Sinclair Ross" continued to divide himself among characters, disguising his "real" self not in the narrator, who bears some notable resemblances, but in the tall, fragile Coulter, whose story-within-a-story is a revealing one somewhat similar to Philip's of shame and withdrawal from a woman. This framing story and the self-destructive tendencies associated with guilt and unrequited love continued to interest Ross, with increasing fatalism. But his "prose" here lacks the urgency of "voice." Of poetry, really. His best stories, as in *The Lamp at Noon*, and his first and last novels, tended to confirm that his imagination was more at home on, and inflamed by, the prairie of his youth. Along with this catalyst went a poet's preference for discontinuous narrative slices: in diary sketches, short stories, monologues and brief scenes evocative of emotional conflict, the natural world, memory.

Was he a novelist? He confessed he found out "too late" his natural talent as a writer was for the novella. From Spain in 1973 he had written to me that he was working on a short novel that "I rather think . . . is 'my' length. . . . I have the wind for a novella. The difference between 250 pages and 125 pages is not 125 — it's getting over the hump and then flogging myself for the rest of the way." You sensed his idea of the novel tended to be synonymous with "prose," and he didn't really trust prose to deliver the "honesty" of style he treasured. (Style, he told me once in Malaga, should be "simple but not flat. Rhythm is important.") He particularly distrusted satirical prose. For some reason it threatened him and aroused his suspicions. "I never understood satire. . . . I get it and I don't get it." He got it; he just didn't like it. It occurs to me it made him feel inferior. I think he associated irony and satire with his mother, but especially with the kind of double life he was always liable to be mocked for: either as a child, "baited" by schoolmates for looking like a sissy and being fatherless, or as a man similarly "baited" and made vulnerable as an "artist" and "queer."

He disliked writers who used satire because it reminded him of the superiority he presumed the author took for granted over a character she was toying with or mocking. This was particularly the case with the writing of his old friend Mavis Gallant, whom he had met in his early days in Montreal. He "admired" her writing "more than he liked it," as he would phrase it about any such work he "didn't get." He once told me an anecdote about a conversation he'd had with Gallant. "You know, Mavis, I admire your writing greatly, but I've never been able to warm to any of your characters." Her amused response? "You who wrote *As for Me and My House* should talk!" He followed her career in *The New Yorker* and could only marvel that someone who'd had the courage to risk throwing up a regular job to devote herself to writing and publishing short stories in the sophisticated cities of Paris and New York, could also make a living at it. Aside from making any money at it, I think this was his own dream when he retired at the age of sixty to try his own luck in Europe.

(A writer closer to his heart was V.S. Pritchett, one of whose stories in *The New Yorker* I think prompted Jim in the summer of 1982 to say he'd like to spend two weeks living by himself on a beach, where he could walk and even ride a horse. We happened to be sitting on a beach. "Neighbors" is about an ageing hairdresser, Lionel Frazier, on his annual walking holiday in Cornwall by the sea. It seemed to me the kind of story Jim might have cared to write himself, were it not all about himself, a man who's had to support his mother much of his life. It flirts with the clichés of homosexuality, loneliness, and the relationship of neighbours, but manages to surprise by the deflection of any expected resolution in a not untypical *New Yorker* story, simply told and effectively observed. The parallels with Jim's life were noticeable — the veiled homosexual, proud of his neat and meticulous independence; the sort of loud, intrusive woman he seemed to attract; his strong worry about intruding neighbours yet anxiety when they *don't* notice him; his good manners and concern over giving offence; his preferred city life with regular hotel holidays elsewhere. But after leaving the prairies Jim never seemed able or interested in writing so close to the bone. By the time he retired to Europe he was still flirting with a world not his own.)

One's first impression of *Whir of Gold* was that he'd smartened up his style since *The Well*. A copy arrived in London where I was living in 1970, with a disarming dedication: "A tearjerker, as I warned you. If you don't use at least one box of Kleenex each I'll know I have failed." We wondered what kind of tears he meant. It sounded more streetwise than the earlier work, if dated, suitable to its Montreal setting, closer to the spoken voice of ellipsis and sketchiness. But sadly it made you want to laugh. It had nothing to say, except perhaps that one's roots in some nebulous way put him in the camp of the psychoanalytical writers, and was particularly coy and cloying about the heterosexual relationship between Sonny and Mad. No more than in his earlier novels could Ross resist, let alone give dramatic resolution to, his real obsession for a homoerotic undertow in which no one, again, happens to dive into it much less drowns. Not unless you count the crime that's planned and executed, and which turns, I think, not very convincingly on the subtext of homosexual initiation. The self-destructive guilt his narrator feels for becoming a popular musician is the same one I think he feels for becoming a heterosexual character.

You sense Ross had grown increasingly conscious in his work of the link between sex, vanity, and violence. But "plot" kept getting in the way. The story "Spike" (1967), for example, was apparently rescued from manuscript pages of a large novel in which the cautious middle-aged family man is presumably unable to find any satisfactory resolution to the unacknowledged problem of his sex life. But this doesn't stop him from picking up hitchhikers, with potentially violent results. (To write of "Sinclair Ross" is to discuss a shadow author of discarded novels that each help to understand his continuing inability to relocate his true voice.) The "criminal mind," which he admitted fascinated him, he associated with consequences and closure — when his natural gifts favoured the obsessive and cyclical. It was as if he sensed that what was "dramatically wrong" with his first novel could be made right by further cultivating his melodramatic tendencies. The "simple clean" style he admired in Isherwood wasn't a prose Jim (or many others) could match. And his homoerotic love was beginning to take its lumps for any fancied liberties. It was as though the author couldn't imagine a less melodramatic way of consummating the love that dared not speak its name: Coulter, escaping a woman, commits suicide; Larson, murdered, is dumped down a well; skinny-armed George is confronted with Spike's knife; the father in "The Flowers That Killed Him" falls off a balcony, murdered by his son; Benny Fox gets punched out in Chicago. It was a dark, pessimistic vision that lurked beneath any fulfilment of passion.

Consider the doctor, Nick Miller, in *Price above Rubies*, illegitimate son of the protagonist in *Sawbones Memorial*. As Ross described this unpublished novel to me, his protagonist is murdered by Caroline Gillespie in revenge for his telling her husband Dunc he was fucking her (also in revenge) for having mocked him and made his life "hell" as a young "hunky." ("Foreigner" is the word he used years before in Athens, when he wanted to know what a woman in Caroline's position would do to such a lover. "She doesn't kill him, does she?" I asked reluctantly. Pause. "You guessed it.") This sequel was to have completed the story of the characters twenty years on, as begun in *Sawbones Memorial*, a novel Jim once described as really being about the protagonist's offstage illegitimate son, Nick. But his publisher turned it down. Murder, revenge, adulterous love. His taste for melodrama gave you pause — though it could also prove arresting, as in "The Painted Door" — and I wish the book could have been published with the dramatis personae and other changes he later talked about inserting to make its reading smoother.

I suspect this work would have revealed his continuing interest in doubles and, by extension, the homoerotic. You conclude that this sentence from *The Well*, describing the young criminal Chris as a lover, might also have applied to the later Nick: "When at last he roused himself and turned upon her to perform as a man, it was almost with a reluctance, a feeling that now he could do no less" (128). Philip and others are embedded in that pronoun of a man whose sexual performances meet more often than not the requirements of society than those of his own body.

His body, yes. Even crippled with Parkinson's disease he didn't give up the obsessions of his male characters easily. Another novel he got rid of, he said, was the one he was writing in Montreal the year before moving to Vancouver: "which common-sense

77

says will go nowhere: a 40-year-old widower with a 17-year-old son who has the mental age of 3. Can you imagine anyone picking a worse subject," he wrote to me. "In plain English, I'm nuts." I vaguely recalled this letter a dozen years later when he began to confide about a "vile" book he'd burned, in which a father takes his retarded son in a wheelchair to a cottage at the lake, where the obliging, good-natured boy commits fellatio on him and then later inadvertently reveals this fact to the town, by pointing to his mouth and saying (something like) "Teddy do." He called this novel *Teddy Do*.

I believe this was the same story he mentioned soon after coming to the West Coast, one which he "once thought of writing," about a father's "shame and guilt" over producing a homosexual son. (These are the same terms, "shame" and "guilt," Mrs. Bentley uses to describe what Philip feels for remaining part of the Church and his motive in adopting his own illegitimate son in order to purge these feelings he wouldn't want his son to see in him.) A few weeks later he'd returned to this theme, saying he'd "thrown out" this book for fear of suddenly dying and having someone discover and try to reconstruct it. He knew the ending was wrong — a surprise the story didn't need — and he thought he could now write it down in a better way. In this account the son is adopted; the father forty-one. It tells of what happens after his wife dies, following the widower's promise to her not to institutionalize the boy but to take care of him instead. Another wet dream?

The reason I'm going into detail about this second unpublished work is because I think it reveals a father-son pattern both characteristic and troubling in Ross's novels and stories. Characteristic because it repeats the Philip-son, Philip-Steve homoerotic scenario in Larson and Chris in *The Well*; in the sex-murderer father whose son tells the story of his funeral and death in "The Flowers That Killed Him"; and in the shame both Coulter's father in "Jug and Bottle" and Benny Fox's father in *Sawbones Memorial* feel over their sons' failure to "measure up to small-town standards" (as Coulter's army friend puts it).

Indeed, as he sometimes said he'd like to do, you might even make a tenuous case for Ross trying to rewrite *As for Me and My House* from Philip's point of view, approximately six years on in *Teddy Do*, having now got rid of the unwelcome wife to permit the dramatic resolution which the subversive theme in the first novel would seem to require. (The ménage à trois in *The Well* got rid of the husband; but it didn't seem to work aesthetically or sexually. In *Price above Rubies* it's the lover who's murdered — I remain in the dark as to what end — and in *Whir of Gold* the ménage à trois, again two men and a woman, has no satisfactory resolution either sexual or artistic. The same could be said for the excerpt from his war novel, "Jug and Bottle," in which Coulter's feeling that he has "killed" (by neglect) the invalid Muriel — the woman he once encouraged with kindness — leads to his suicide and the narrator's fateful discovery that he's similarly responsible for killing Coulter.) You might argue the obsessions of the author's body tended to repeat themselves in the fictional patterns of his mind. Especially when considering how the father-son pattern is not only characteristic but also troubling, because of its incestuous and even pedophilic overtones.

Here we arrive in the moral vicinity of Norman Douglas and Lawrence Durrell, both Mediterranean expatriate writers, the first whose penchant for young boys was known during his lifetime and the other whose alleged incest with his daughter became known after his death. I'm not suggesting Jim's infatuation with "boys" was quite an underage one, but he did have a curious tolerance for clergy and others accused in the press of abusing children, occasionally saying to me how flirtatious children could invite this sort of sexual attraction and how they must "enjoy it." Otherwise, "you have to wonder how it could go on. The child could always say no." On this same visit I heard him postulate the naked father — and how the son, used to seeing his penis, wasn't going to reject out of hand the father's approaches. Indeed, Arab boys had seen one another naked so often a stranger's penis wasn't going to shock them.

Jim didn't believe children were the "innocent" victims they were made out to be, and that boys were impressed by the attention of a man. He didn't seem to buy into any current notion of moral thinking about prey and the preyed-upon. Recent public condemnation of child abuse in the Maritimes he felt had been blown out of proportion. He wasn't a pedophile, he said, preferring boys when they "started to get rough" — what I took to mean adolescent. Steve's age. A fine line you might think for anything but sublimation or Nabokov's Humbert Humbert. And yet a line he confessed twice to me of crossing in Tenerife, where he once slept with a hotel manager's son, "twelve or so," who "made me work" the night he couldn't find accommodation elsewhere. Whether the story was true or not, its expression of desire was certainly genuine.

The theme of our conversation had been fathers and sons — how sons would supposedly take him home to their fathers after having sex with Jim. The son would also have sex with the father he said. He was repeating another story, from his Barcelona days. Again, whether true or not doesn't matter so much as how these reported trysts tended to confirm an obsession of the older man in his writings for a younger one, and how the father figure often seems intimately involved in the resultant ménage à trois. In "The Flowers That Killed Him" (1972) this obsession finally finds a resolution of sorts in a strange and densely mirrored story of two funerals, one for the second boy-victim recently murdered, the other for the tall father responsible for these murders of his son's friends from the school where the father was principal. The father dies by "falling" from his apartment balcony, five stories to his death, pushed by his son. In this last of his published short stories, it's now the *son* feeling shame and guilt for the father. It's in this story where the father figure is finally "killed off," as it were, and exorcised (however much he tended to linger on in the unpublished *Teddy Do* — also about shaming the father).

The "criminal mind" that Ross said interested him was, of course, his own mind. And it was intimately caught up, not in the forthright mind of his mother but in the brooding mind of his father — the parent *I* think he felt more a part of his own being and destiny. "It's useless wondering if I'd have turned out the way I did . . . ," he once related — if his father's outgoing personality hadn't suddenly changed after a serious fall, injuring his head when he fell from a runaway democrat, causing him over time to grow violent and abusive towards his wife. This was the fall that eventually prompted his mother to leave home with Jim as a child. (He was telling me this in hospital after his own second fall in Vancouver; dwelling on his father, whom his mother dismissed as "a lumber-jack." "It's odd the things that happen. And then the son comes along and writes a novel to account for it.") I think in his laconic way he was alluding to his belief in the nurture side of the nurture-nature debate, about the origins of his homosexuality.

It seemed somehow archetypal that a "fall" for him should have associations of sin, disgrace, and vio-lence. (His fear of falling in the street was wrapped up in the shame he felt with Parkinson's.) As for his first violent fall in Vancouver — in his attempt to kill himself — that he should have associated this fall the next day with the disgrace of a Spanish politician who "fell" into ruin for giving in to the temptations of a young boy, repeats rather a complex pattern too revealing to ignore. And I've sometimes wondered if Jim's story about his father's fall wasn't an elaborate protective fiction he or his mother had worked up or embellished to cover something deeper, perhaps to do with some bodily abuse of him as a child he may have experienced or simply perceived. (He told me his first sexual interest occurred when he was very young and attracted to a very tall "boy," about six foot six, who paid him no attention.)

His defence of child molesters in conversations was certainly odd. And his empathy for tall, somewhat strange characters, such as his father had turned out to be, seems more than "idealizing" if one were to carry this notion of incest another step and to see something of its recurrence in the son's attitudes — if not his behaviour — evidently not an uncommon occurrence among those abused as children. In this regard, it's interesting to read Doc Hunter's account of the abortion he performed on the eighteen-year-old daughter of a farmer whose child she was about to have. Hunter refuses to condemn the incest and tries to understand the relationship.

(About incest I should perhaps add that in a conversation with Jim the morning after his arrival in Vancouver, in 1982, he observed how incest seemed a more commonplace literary theme these days and how the taboo around it looked to be disappearing now that women could take the birth control pill and men use a condom. In other words, wherein the harm? He seemed totally outside the usual bounds of morality in this regard. Perhaps like his character, the doctor, his refusal to condemn sexual misconduct of any kind was more an attempt to understand it.)

By the time he came to live in Spain in the early 1970s, Jim Ross was familiar with the Mediterranean, for he had once adopted a boy in Italy through what he called a "corrupt" international foster plan. Perhaps it was around the time my wife and I were thinking of adopting a daughter in Sri Lanka through a similar plan — at the beach in Vancouver one late July, during a golden sunset, the tide in flood, young men standing on the swimming raft drinking beer — when he began to narrate his own experience as a foster parent. He was feeling open and relaxed. He would later recite some Tennyson. He told us how he'd sent money and letters for the boy, until, upon his first visit to Salvatore's family in a shanty suburb of Naples, he discovered neither his money nor letters had been getting through. He had found his way to his son's house without much trouble, but was disconcerted by the dirt and chocolate running out of the children's mouths. Over the following years Jim kept up a direct correspondence with the boy, thus preventing the agency from creaming off his cheques.

The next time he visited Italy the family picked him up at his hotel in a car, taking him home for dinner. By now Salvatore was sixteen and taller than his foster father. During dinner there was a knock at the door, which his real father got up to answer, and began carrying on a conversation in a Neapolitan dialect Jim couldn't really follow, but understood that the father was required to come up with a large sum of money, perhaps $500. "Oh no you don't," he thought to himself. "What kind of a sucker do you take me for?" Feeling certain he was being set up, by a father who hadn't been around during his first visit, Ross gathered his wits, and when driven back to his hotel, where Salvatore followed him up to his room, Jim simply turned at the door and offered to shake his hand. That was the last time he saw his adopted son. At this age the boy seemed old enough to support himself. The father, he told us, had simply ruined things.

This anecdote is imbued with certain recurrent obsessions: the boy, the fatherless boy, the father; risking self and money through a characteristic credulity Jim feared in himself; and his growing disillusion with "finding someone out" as an excuse to drop them from his moral high ground suddenly gained. The pattern of shame and guilt between a father and his son was not easily expiated.

The Mediterranean seemed to represent for Ross the exotic place of ideal love, even erotic longing, as though he'd first been attracted there through the dark, gypsyish features of Steve, the vigorous Catholic boy at the other extreme from his own puny Protestant childhood on the Canadian prairie (cf. Philip's). At the same time Steve seemed a character redolent of himself in the imagined disadvantages of orphanhood, impoverishment, and the need of a father. But the nature of exotic and ideal love, as first embodied in Philip's attraction to Steve, meant any such yearning was doomed to disillusionment instead of fulfillment. It was doomed to bathos.

It was only in its art, in the works of Lorca, say, or in the museums full of the paintings of Goya or

El Greco, that Ross found his ideal love for the Mediterranean uncorrupted and transcendent. It was in the cinemas, on the other hand, where he found it corrupted beyond his fictional imaginings in the transgressive gropes and fleeting trysts with strangers. This, sadly, was the love he came to think of (in relating it increasingly to me) as the only kind of testament possible to his intimate desires. The value of art faded as his stock in the body rose. Perhaps he was never in love, or never loved another person in his life, except for his mother when he was very young, and his father, if at all, in a contradictory romantic way bound up in the shame of no longer having a father.

I think Jim wondered all his life what love was. He had trouble showing approval, admiration, affection — not least of and for himself. I recall visiting him in his nursing home — the same day, incidentally, he revealed that he'd tried to commit suicide years before when I found him in the sandwich shop — and he was saying how he'd been lying in bed last night reciting poetry when he couldn't sleep. I asked if he'd ever written any poetry. "A little." And he began to recite in a weak, halting voice three rhyming stanzas he happened to have been writing in his head. "Love is an oxymoron . . ." it began. The second stanza started, "Love is hyperbole . . ." And the third verse had a Yeatsian flavour, "Love is a palace . . ." in which "phallus" rhymed with "palace," I remember, and the word "excrement" appeared. "I must write it out," he said.

Love, it must be said, seemed beyond him if only

by his own obsessive definitions. Love was a contradiction in terms, an impossible exaggeration, an unattainable ideal. "I had lots of opportunities to meet people," he once ruefully reflected, listening to my account of a fortieth anniversary banquet for a homosexual couple, friends of ours I'd introduced him to some years earlier. "I turned them down." It's no wonder he never found love except in art, and rarely in his own fiction, where lovelessness generally governed. That his work always failed to win him the love he expected it should have, that it failed to win him the fame and fortune represented in his own mind most powerfully by the Royal Bank prize, embittered him. (In regard to that prestigious cash award, he didn't think he had never won it because he'd "liked the boys," since he'd always been "careful" when he worked for the bank. He just couldn't account for the failure of this honour to come his way, especially as a noted former employee, and he dwelled on it unhealthily.)

He desired love and recognition and found it by proxy in the retirement reception for old Doc Hunter in *Sawbones Memorial*, a novel that should have won the Governor General's Award for fiction in 1975. Not until this last published novel did he come back so successfully to "voice" — and this time with a vengeance. The whole novel was voice: dialogues and monologues, interior and otherwise, without a comment or interjection from a narrator or author. It was a tour de force, catalyzed by Claude Mauriac's novel *Dîner en Ville*, in which dialogue alone serves to advance the story of several characters talking round a dinner table. (I always counted among the films he enjoyed most in Vancouver *My Dinner with André*, an endless-seeming discussion between two men in a New York restaurant. The notion here of talking attracted him more than any of the ideas discussed. He'd lived most of his life alone, knowing few people he could really talk to, and sometimes startled you by asking how to pronounce a word like "charisma," which he'd read but never heard, or by using an expression like "having a piece of tail" when it seemed dated or entirely out of place.) *Sawbones*, by eschewing plot and prose, as it were, regained the ground of his earliest and most powerful novel in which the narrator's voice was itself the story in the manner of its yearning.

Except now his preoccupations transcended the limited personal relationship of a couple in order to broaden his canvas to a whole town, and with the sixties having loosened up acceptable tastes, he was able to look back to the forties and even write about the queer Benny Fox in an explicit way without worrying much about disturbing his own false front. He was now far away in Spain. (This also allowed him to publish "The Flowers That Killed Him" two years earlier, another very "voicey" story though too compressed and over-plotted to arouse much empathy in the reader.) He felt free to write frankly about incest, suicide, adultery, and prejudice in a small town far from its gossip. He had become the purveyor himself of gossip, making up a novel out of secrets and relaxing into their fears and obsessions. From the farmhouses of his earliest tight-lipped stories he'd ended up in a hospital full of reminiscent voices.

Shortly after he arrived in Vancouver I asked him if the wind that lifts the house and carries it off in *The Wizard of Oz* had at all influenced the wind and house in *As for Me and My House*. "Oh, probably," he replied. And I thought that was the amusing end of it. I knew he hated wind. But he must have given it some more thought, because the next time I saw him he wanted to talk about *Oz*, a book he'd read at the age of nine. "I'm afraid I missed the point. The highlight for me was the cyclone. I found the fantasy land after that a letdown. I was disappointed that the wizard turned out to be a little old man."

I think the fatherless Jim was always looking for the tall ideal wizard. Who he found at the end of the road, after tall Philip Bentley in the beginning, was little old Doc Hunter, a worthy wizard and role model of sorts, but a compromised one. Which is part of the reason for Hunter's success as a character: no authorial illusions. And ironically he's straight, no underlying homoerotic yearnings that one can detect to retard dramatic development, a kind of politically incorrect doctor who isn't above taking advantage of women patients. Moreover, he's the only adult male protagonist of any depth in Ross's fiction who really carries our conviction as readers. It was as though in removing his own false front as a writer, and emerging frankly about the secondary Benny Fox in this novel, he was also able to come to artistic terms with the complicated self in "Sinclair Ross" through the one professional he idealized — the doctor.

(He'd earlier considered using a retiring teacher and a banker but discarded these.) The medical profession allowed him to be more honest, I think, about the bodily world, and about how ideals play out in the larger social world where an artist like Philip was unable to survive and had no place.

Jim may have been radical and subversive in his thinking about sex, but when talking about this larger social world he was a self-reliant man of his generation. Not that he talked about it much. His social conscience wasn't particularly encompassing and he kept his money mainly away from the coffers of charity. It was as though he had to keep up the appearance of straitened circumstances, when in fact he was comfortably well off. Conservative and even reactionary, though rarely opinionated, he disliked welfare support and abortion on demand. He admitted that his Puritan streak didn't allow him to feel much sympathy for panhandlers or alcoholics (Malcolm Lowry's drunken consul was among these). Loss of self-control distressed him. He thought men should cure themselves of their vices and not rely on others. For such an empathetic chronicler of the dustbowl years, he'd made sure the great Depression hadn't turned him into a socialist. ("I didn't notice it," he once said. "I had my job." Indeed men in breadlines never appeared in yarns about his first three-week trip to New York, which included a nightclub and the opera, nor about his second trip there a couple of years later which took in the Turkish baths and buying sex. Chicago he remembered for happy boxing fans in the street and for good sex with four boys along the lakeshore.) He liked obedient children, social and political stability — to the extent of living without too many qualms under a Greek junta as well as under Franco — and he used to dislike radical students and especially "hangers-on." Yet he was no fan of Spiro Agnew, I remember, and refused to condemn "the nattering nabobs of negativism" immortalized by Agnew. He could be persuaded by editorials in the *The New Yorker* and by James Reston's columns in the *International Herald Tribune*. He rather admired Pierre Trudeau for wanting to keep the state out of the bedrooms of the nation; and he always had a soft spot for the little guy in Jean Chrétien.

I still see him, short halting steps down Comox Street, allowing himself to pause at the urging of a friend under the pink flowering cherry blossoms, in the small square at Chilco, two years to the day of his arrival in Vancouver, before pushing on to the "little Israeli" restaurant on Denman where he was known by the dark handsome waiter. Waiters were also his wizards, because for years they had fed his imagination, lonely for ideal male figures.

Casting back further I see him taking short halting steps along the railway platform toward me that spring day in 1982, when he arrived in Vancouver overdressed in his overcoat, tie, and a pearl-gray fedora, a little old man out of the 1930s, the only time I ever saw him wear a hat, now in my son's forgotten dress-up box. Paul Kirby wears a similar pearl-gray fedora in the first novel, looking sheepish and somewhat out of place according to Mrs.

Bentley, "like a farmer at a picnic in his Sunday best."

The size of Jim's head was small, the way his tall hero's heads are also small, and yet the size of his brain was disproportionately large. It was the brain of a "simple fellow," he misleadingly believed, who was more a maker than a thinker: "I've read some of the prescribed books," as the narrator of "Jug and Bottle" tells us, "but my interests have always run to people and things, rather than to values and ideas. I like tools and tinkering." Typewriters and revisions, he might have added, keyboards and practice, and, until the age of eighteen, canvas and brushstrokes.

But this wasn't the whole picture. If Jim wasn't always sound on "values and ideas," his interests certainly ran that way in his omnivorous reading. He read and admired both Spender the critic and Isherwood the novelist. Having divided himself so much in his fiction, he came to embody for me both the skinniness and idealism of Don Quixote and the shortness and adulteration of Sancho Panza. It's no wonder he came to find in Spain, in spite of its dictatorship when he settled there, a country that brought him his most happiness as a man and where he wrote well. He travelled widely in Spain ("Speaking of the Spanish landscape," he'd written to me from Barcelona in 1971, "between Madrid and Toledo it's exactly — yes, *exactly* — like Saskatchewan"), and from Spain had made trips to Morocco, back to London for the first time since the war, to the Canary Islands and Majorca, and to various cities in Europe. He was appalled at the mass tourism Spain encouraged — little umbrellas tied to the buggy horses' heads in Malaga he found "disgraceful!" — and yet he was always curious about people with their many foibles, looking upon them, as it were, from a quixotic height he never quite understood except through the short Panza's appetite for the earthy.

I remember him at his most relaxed one summer's day in Malaga in 1975, high in his top-floor apartment along Paseo Maritimo, overlooking the Mediterranean from a narrow balcony twelve stories up. He looked younger than he had in Athens,[*] urbane and in good humour, wearing a tan shirt and trousers, a pair of tan canvas shoes with no socks. His Meccano-like metal bookcases ranged behind us, which included several books on Freud. We were having drinks, watching the freighters at anchor. He was talking in his light tenor voice, openly of his family, in a way he'd been reluctant to do in Athens. *Sawbones Memorial* had been critically acclaimed the year before. Recently, he'd been reading Yeats. He talked of Rimbaud and Baudelaire. Even of Norman Douglas and *South Wind* which he'd once enjoyed. A year or two earlier he'd travelled through Morocco and was full of a tourist's tales about his encounter with the Third World. He quoted a Walter Scott poem about the traveller who hates his native land, and applied this jovially to himself. In Spanish he was reading both Lorca and Frederick Forsyth, whose

---

[*] Perhaps his facelift had helped my perception here?

The Day of the Jackal he couldn't put down. He spoke of the Spanish and Gibraltar. Of Rembrandt whom he didn't like and El Greco whom he did. ("There's something far more religious about his painting than religion — if that makes sense.") He seemed chock-a-block full of happy preferences. Not so long ago in the Netherlands he'd heard Beethoven's Eighth, which had never appealed to him; more attractive to him had been a Bruckner Seventh in Madrid some time earlier. His favourite dog was a German shepherd. Mention of Julian Huxley's *Memoirs* reminded him of attending Huxley's lecture on bugs, in Winnipeg before the war.

It was either in his apartment, or at lunch another day even higher up, on the terrace of the Parador, amid the hot pines and hibiscus overlooking the bullring and city, that he admitted he was thinking of moving to another apartment. He didn't like the thin walls and noisiness of his "neighbours."

Perhaps things weren't quite so ideal as they seemed. The "humiliation" of the infirmities associated with age were beginning to worry him. He talked at length about prostate problems and the hepatitis he'd contracted many years before in Montreal. (In later years I always thought of this restaurant as the one where he said he first noticed his Parkinsonian tremor, at lunch one day trying to pour red wine for a friend. Usually wine was a kind of elixir for him, a symbol of rejuvenation. He hadn't had his first glass till the age of fifty, on his first trip to Mexico City.) At Caso Pedro, another restaurant closer to the sea, he seemed older and more vulnerable. A characteristic palm across his bald forehead would rub there as he spoke or listened, the middle finger raised as though about to press a sticky key on the cornet.

Yet delighted with the conversation he could still cock his arm at a right angle, holding the back of his chair. He liked Jack Nicholson and Malcolm McDowell. He was willing to go out on a limb and say his favourite among his own stories was "A Circus in Town." (He always tended to prefer work he'd written relatively fast, such as this story, or the memoir of his mother, and his first and last published novels. The quality of his work seemed to diminish in ratio to the years he laboured over it.) Of bomb alerts in High Holborn during the war he recalled the sudden "array of posteriors" visible under desks at Army Headquarters. On another evening, walking the streets in Torremolinos after dinner, he remembered how much these street women in their forties, made up to look hard and self-sufficient, used to bother him in Barcelona. He *hated* this. I think it was their independence that bothered him.

On one such evening he also spoke of feuding parents. "The worst thing is when they quarrel and the children suffer." And then later, after more red wine and distant years summarized, this: "There's a sentence in Hemingway that for me sums up the whole human condition. It's in the novel set in Italy . . . *A Farewell to Arms*. It's very simple," he said, pointing in the air to each of the words. " 'You suffer, and you make suffer.' "

I still don't know if these words are in Hemingway's novel or not. My guess is they are. But years later in a Vancouver restaurant, also by the sea, having just read a new edition of Hemingway's war novel, my friend swore they had been removed.